OVERVIEW-MAP KEY

● ●

:: FLORIDA PANHANDLE 7

1 Big Lagoon State Park Campground 8
2 Blackwater River State Park Campground 11
3 Camel Lake Campground 14
4 Dead Lakes Park Campground 17
5 Falling Waters State Park Campground 20
6 Florida Caverns State Park Campground 23
7 Grayton Beach State Park Campground 26
8 High Bluff Campground 29
9 Ochlockonee River State Park Campground 32
10 Pine Log State Forest Campground 35
11 Rocky Bayou State Park Campground 38
12 St. Andrews State Park Campground 41
13 St. George Island State Park Campground 44
14 St. Joseph Peninsula State Park Campground 47
15 Torreya State Park Campground 50
16 Wright Lake Recreation Area Campground 53

:: NORTHERN FLORIDA 57

17 Anastasia State Park Campground 58
18 Fort Clinch State Park Campground 61
19 Gold Head Branch State Park Campground 64
20 Hammock Campground at Jennings State Forest 67
21 Little Talbot Island State Park Campground 70
22 Manatee Springs State Park Campground 73
23 O'Leno State Park Campground 76
24 Ocean Pond Campground 79
25 Paynes Prairie Preserve State Park Campground 82
26 Suwannee River State Park Campground 85

:: CENTRAL FLORIDA 89

27 Alexander Springs Recreation Area Campground 90
28 Blue Spring State Park Campground 93
29 Chassahowitzka River Campground: Indian Ridge Loop 96
30 Clearwater Lake Campground 99
31 Hillsborough River State Park Campground 102
32 Hog Island Recreation Area Campground 105
33 Hopkins Prairie Campground 108
34 Juniper Springs Recreation Area Campground 111
35 Lake Eaton Campground 114
36 Lithia Springs Park Campground 117
37 Mutual Mine Recreation Area Campground 120
38 Starkey Wilderness Park Campground 123

:: SOUTH FLORIDA 126

39 Bahia Honda State Park Campground 127
40 Bear Island Campground 130
41 Caloosahatchee Regional Park Campground 133
42 Cayo Costa State Park Campground 136
43 DuPuis Campground 139
44 Elliott Key Campground 142
45 Flamingo Campground 145
46 John Pennekamp Coral Reef State Park Campground 148
47 Jonathan Dickinson State Park Campground 151
48 Long Key State Park Campground 154
49 Long Pine Key Campground 157
50 Oscar Scherer State Park Campground 160

Florida Campground Locator Map

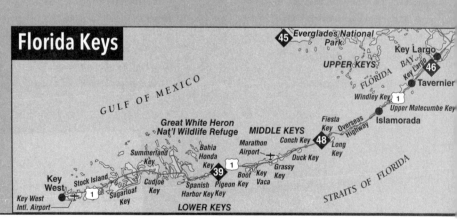

Florida Keys

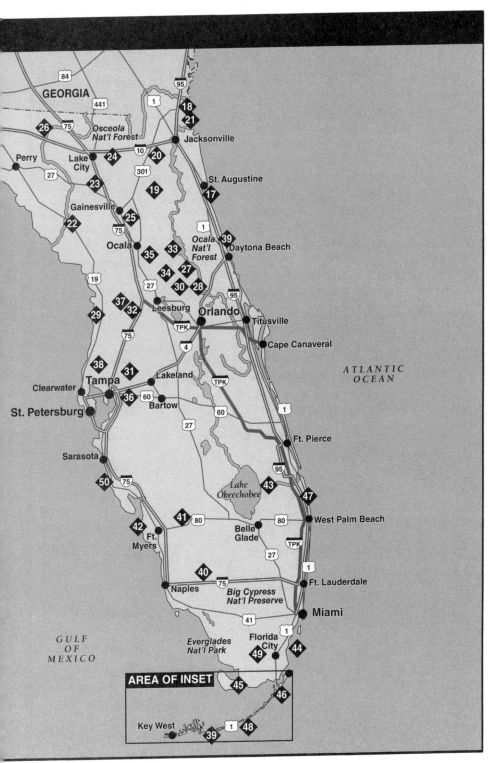

Florida Campground Map Legend

 North indicator

→ Off-map or pinpoint-indication arrow

△ Campground name and location

Individual tent sites, RV sites, and equestrian sites

△△ Group site

 Tallahassee ✪ Capital

Crestview ● City or town

NATIONAL FOREST STATE PARK Public lands

Main Trail **Hiking and equestrian trails**

━65━ Interstate highways

━319━90━ US highways

━30E━78━ State roads

Bond Falls Rd Other roads

Dirt/gravel roads

Boardwalk

Wire fence

Ferry route

Blackwater River River or stream

Wright Lake Lake or pond

≍ Bridge or tunnel	Playground	🟖 Picnic area
Amphitheater	P Parking	Sheltered picnic area
Water access	Marina or boat ramp	Dump station
Wheelchair accessible	(Telephone	Fire pit
Restroom	Swimming	Fishing area
Pit toilet	Ranger station	Gate
Trash disposal	Canoe put-in	Showers
Store	Gazebo	Outside shower
Restaurant	Laundry	$ Pay station
Historic fort	Tower	† Cemetery
(?) Information	▲ Peak	Lodging
Recycle bin	No swimming	Corral
Firewood	Stables	

BEST TENT CAMPING

FLORIDA

FIFTH EDITION

:: OTHER TITLES IN THE SERIES:

Best Tent Camping: The Carolinas

Best Tent Camping: Colorado

Best Tent Camping: Georgia

Best Tent Camping: Illinois

Best Tent Camping: Kentucky

Best Tent Camping: Maryland

Best Tent Camping: Michigan

Best Tent Camping: Minnesota

Best Tent Camping: Missouri and
   the Ozarks

Best Tent Camping: Montana

Best Tent Camping: New England

Best Tent Camping: New Jersey

Best Tent Camping: New Mexico

Best Tent Camping: New York State

Best Tent Camping:
   Northern California

Best Tent Camping: Ohio

Best Tent Camping: Oregon

Best Tent Camping: Pennsylvania

Best Tent Camping: The Southern
   Appalachian and Smoky Mountains

Best Tent Camping: Southern California

Best Tent Camping: Tennessee

Best Tent Camping: Texas

Best Tent Camping: Utah

Best Tent Camping: Virginia

Best Tent Camping: Washington

Best Tent Camping: West Virginia

Best Tent Camping: Wisconsin

BEST TENT CAMPING

FLORIDA

YOUR CAR-CAMPING GUIDE TO SCENIC BEAUTY, THE SOUNDS OF NATURE, AND AN ESCAPE FROM CIVILIZATION

Fifth Edition

JOHNNY MOLLOY

MENASHA RIDGE PRESS
Your Guide to the Outdoors Since 1982

:: *This book is for Hunt Cochrane, a fair canoer, a good camper, a better backpacker, and a great friend.*

Best Tent Camping: Florida, 5th Edition

Copyright © 2016 by Johnny Molloy
All rights reserved
Printed in the United States of America
Published by Menasha Ridge Press
Distributed by Publishers Group West
Fifth edition, first printing

Cataloging-in-Publication Data is available from the Library of Congress

Cover design by Scott McGrew
Cover photo © Greg Gard / Alamy Stock Photo
Text design by Annie Long
Cartography by Steve Jones and Johnny Molloy
Indexing by Rich Carlson

 Menasha Ridge Press
2204 First Avenue S., Suite 102
Birmingham, Alabama 35233
menasharidge.com

CONTENTS

• •

Overview-Map Key i

Florida Campground Locator Map . . . . ii–iii

Map Legend iv

Best Campgrounds xi

Acknowledgments xiii

Preface xiv

Introduction 1

:: FLORIDA PANHANDLE 7

1 Big Lagoon State Park Campground 8

2 Blackwater River State Park Campground 11

3 Camel Lake Campground 14

4 Dead Lakes Park Campground 17

5 Falling Waters State Park Campground 20

6 Florida Caverns State Park Campground 23

7 Grayton Beach State Park Campground 26

8 High Bluff Campground 29

9 Ochlockonee River State Park Campground 32

10 Pine Log State Forest Campground 35

11 Rocky Bayou State Park Campground 38

12 St. Andrews State Park Campground 41

13 St. George Island State Park Campground 44

14 St. Joseph Peninsula State Park Campground 47

15 Torreya State Park Campground 50

16 Wright Lake Recreation Area Campground 53

:: NORTHERN FLORIDA 57

17 Anastasia State Park Campground 58

18 Fort Clinch State Park Campground 61

19 Gold Head Branch State Park Campground 64

20 Hammock Campground at Jennings State Forest 67

21 Little Talbot Island State Park Campground 70

22 Manatee Springs State Park Campground 73

23 O'Leno State Park Campground 76

24 Ocean Pond Campground 79

25 Paynes Prairie Preserve State Park Campground 82

26 Suwannee River State Park Campground 85

:: CENTRAL FLORIDA 89

27 Alexander Springs Recreation Area Campground 90
28 Blue Spring State Park Campground. 93
29 Chassahowitzka River Campground: Indian Ridge Loop 96
30 Clearwater Lake Campground 99
31 Hillsborough River State Park Campground 102
32 Hog Island Recreation Area Campground 105
33 Hopkins Prairie Campground 108
34 Juniper Springs Recreation Area Campground. 111
35 Lake Eaton Campground. 114
36 Lithia Springs Park Campground 117
37 Mutual Mine Recreation Area Campground 120
38 Starkey Wilderness Park Campground 123

:: SOUTH FLORIDA 126

39 Bahia Honda State Park Campground 127
40 Bear Island Campground. 130
41 Caloosahatchee Regional Park Campground 133
42 Cayo Costa State Park Campground. 136
43 DuPuis Campground 139
44 Elliott Key Campground 142
45 Flamingo Campground 145
46 John Pennekamp Coral Reef State Park Campground. 148
47 Jonathan Dickinson State Park Campground 151
48 Long Key State Park Campground. 154
49 Long Pine Key Campground. 157
50 Oscar Scherer State Park Campground 160

:: APPENDIXES AND INDEX 163

Appendix A: Camping-Equipment Checklist. 163
Appendix B: Sources of Information 164
Index 165
About the Author 169

BEST CAMPGROUNDS

:: BEST CAMPGROUNDS FOR FISHING

1 Big Lagoon State Park Campground (page 8)

11 Rocky Bayou State Park Campground (page 38)

18 Fort Clinch State Park Campground (page 61)

29 Chassahowitzka River Campground: Indian Ridge Loop (page 96)

:: BEST CAMPGROUNDS FOR HIKING

3 Camel Lake Campground (page 14)

33 Hopkins Prairie Campground (page 108)

37 Mutual Mine Recreation Area Campground (page 120)

38 Starkey Wilderness Park Campground (page 123)

47 Jonathan Dickinson State Park Campground (page 151)

:: BEST CAMPGROUNDS FOR BICYCLERS

22 Manatee Springs State Park Campground (page 73)

30 Clearwater Lake Campground (page 99)

42 Cayo Costa State Park Campground (page 136)

45 Flamingo Campground (page 145)

49 Long Pine Key Campground (page 157)

:: BEST CAMPGROUNDS FOR PADDLING

27 Alexander Springs Recreation Area Campground (page 90)

31 Hillsborough River State Park Campground (page 102)

34 Juniper Springs Recreation Area Campground (page 111)

36 Lithia Springs Park Campground (page 117)

45 Flamingo Campground (page 145)

:: BEST CAMPGROUNDS FOR WILDLIFE WATCHING

19 Gold Head Branch State Park Campground (page 64)

20 Hammock Campground at Jennings State Forest (page 67)

22 Manatee Springs State Park Campground (page 73)

25 Paynes Prairie Preserve State Park Campground (page 82)

28 Blue Spring State Park Campground (page 93)

49 Long Pine Key Campground (page 157)

:: BEST CAMPGROUNDS FOR SOLITUDE

4 Dead Lakes Park Campground (page 17)

8 High Bluff Campground (page 29)

15 Torreya State Park Campground (page 50)

40 Bear Island Campground (page 130)

43 DuPuis Campground (page 139)

:: BEST LAKE CAMPGROUNDS

10 Pine Log State Forest Campground (page 35)

16 Wright Lake Recreation Area Campground (page 53)

24 Ocean Pond Campground (page 79)

35 Lake Eaton Campground (page 114)

37 Mutual Mine Recreation Area Campground (page 120)

:: BEST RIVER CAMPGROUNDS

2 Blackwater River State Park Campground (page 11)

:: BEST RIVER CAMPGROUNDS
(CONTINUED)

9   Ochlockonee River State Park
Campground (page 32)

26 Suwannee River State Park
Campground (page 85)

32 Hog Island Recreation Area
Campground (page 105)

50 Oscar Scherer State Park Campground
(page 160)

BEST BEACH CAMPGROUNDS

7   Grayton Beach State Park Campground
(page 26)

12 St. Andrews State Park Campground
(page 41)

14 St. Joseph Peninsula State Park
Campground (page 47)

39 Bahia Honda State Park Campground
(page 127)

48 Long Key State Park Campground
(page 154)

BEST ISLAND CAMPGROUNDS

13 St. George Island State Park
Campground (page 44)

32 Hog Island Recreation Area
Campground (page 105)

42 Cayo Costa State Park Campground
(page 136)

44 Elliott Key Campground
(page 142)

ACKNOWLEDGMENTS

● ●

Updating the fifth edition of this book was an adventure in itself. Along the way I met old friends and new. I learned a lot and received help from many people. Thanks to my wife, Keri Anne, who has explored all over the Sunshine State with me, Pam Morgan, Skip Krassa, The Pole from Baltimore, Eddie Duval, J. L. Plummer, Lisa Daniel, Irv Edwards, Anthony Lauria, Ranger Julie Watson, Barbara and Eve of Cayo Costa, Roger Chubin, George Drinnon, Nelle Molloy, Maggie Bryars, Brian Babb, Meredith Morris-Babb, and Tom Lauria.

I thank all the Florida state park and state forest employees who helped me out, as well as all other public servants who endured my endless questions.

Finally, a special thanks goes to Hunt Cochrane, Kim Breasseale, David Zaczyk, John and Barb Haapala, Aaron Marable, and all the campers who love wild Florida as much as I do.

PREFACE

• •

Welcome to the fifth edition of *Best Tent Camping: Florida*. This book has undergone a complete updating, including the addition of new campgrounds! Florida is well known as a vacation getaway for those weary of northern winters—those who are seeking a tropical atmosphere and oceanside ambience. A century ago, the Sunshine State was a sleepy, agricultural land of orange groves and cattle ranches. Since then, it has seen the rise of the urban landscape, as winter visitors made Florida their permanent home. Vacationers continue to come to the area, enjoying the cities as much as the climate. Modern times have seen the development of man-made attractions that have become destinations in their own right.

Florida continues to grow. Fortunately for us, state and federal governments have intervened to preserve the natural beauty of the land, the same beauty encountered by Ponce de Leon's men as they searched for the Fountain of Youth. They didn't realize it at the time, but the Spaniards were traversing some of the most lush and unique landscapes in what would later become the United States. New preserved lands have opened new camping destinations included in this book, including DuPuis Campground in the pines near Lake Okeechobee.

Today, we can still see what Ponce de Leon saw: rolling sand hills of the central ridge, sugar-white beaches of the Gulf Coast, vast mangrove stands of the Everglades, incredible rivers of all lengths and varieties, pine flatwoods whose needles perfume the air. This is what the Division of State Parks likes to call "the real Florida."

After you have explored some of this state's natural preserves, new images of Florida will emerge: not only Miami's South Beach but also the blue water of the Keys; not only Disney World but also Clearwater Lake; not only Cape Canaveral but the federal batteries at Fort Clinch. Your revised picture of Florida will include the human history of Florida: aboriginal Floridians exploring crystalline Lithia Springs; "Cracker" cowboys running cattle at the DuPuis Ranch, now a wildlife preserve; and citizens banding together to stop "Spite Highway" on Elliott Key.

This book will also open your eyes to the vast recreation opportunities extending throughout the state, whether you are hiking the Florida Trail near Ocean Pond, paddling the Withlacoochee River at Hog Island, bird-watching at Flamingo, or shelling at Cayo Costa Island. With this book in hand, you will be able to combine your camping experience with memorable outdoor adventures.

A fine tent-camping experience will enhance your knowledge of Florida. I combed the state in search of the best outdoors combination: fine tent camping coupled with interesting scenic locales. My problem was picking only the 50 best campgrounds. Whether you are a native Floridian in search of new territory or an out-of-state vacationer, this book will help you unlock the secrets to the real, natural Florida.

—Johnny Molloy

INTRODUCTION

● ●

How to Use This Guidebook

:: THE RATING SYSTEM

Included in this book is a rating system for Florida's 50 best campgrounds. Certain campground attributes—beauty, privacy, spaciousness, quiet, security, and cleanliness—are ranked using a star system. Each campground in this guidebook is superlative in its own way. For example, a site may be rated only one star in one category but perhaps five stars in another category. This rating system allows you to choose your destination based on the attributes that are most important to you. Though these ratings are subjective, they're still excellent guidelines for finding the perfect camping experience for you and your companions.

★ ★ ★ ★ ★ The site is **ideal** in that category.

★ ★ ★ ★ The site is **exemplary** in that category.

★ ★ ★ The site is **very good** in that category.

★ ★ The site is **above average** in that category.

★ The site is **acceptable** in that category.

Beauty

In the best campgrounds, the fluid shapes of nature—flora, water, land, and sky—have melded to create locales that seem to have been made for tent camping. The best sites are so attractive you may be tempted not to leave your outdoor home. A little site work is all right to make the scenic area camper friendly, but too many reminders of civilization eliminated many a campground from inclusion in this book.

Privacy

A little understory goes a long way in making you feel comfortable once you've picked your site for the night. There is a trend of planting natural borders between campsites if the borders don't already exist. With some trees or brush to define the sites, every camper has personal space. Then you can go about the pleasures of tent camping without keeping up with the Joneses at the next site over—or them with you.

Spaciousness

This attribute can be very important depending on how much of a gearhead you are and the size of your group. Campers with family-style tents need a large, flat spot on which to pitch their tent and still get to the ice chest to prepare foods, all the while not getting burned near the fire ring. Gearheads need adequate space to show off all of their stuff to the neighbors strolling by. I just want enough room to keep my bedroom, kitchen, and den separate.

Quiet

Nature's symphony—waves lapping against the shore, singing birds, wind rushing through the pines, and thunderstorms passing in the night—is the kind of noise tent campers associate with being in Florida. In concert, they camouflage the sounds you don't want to hear: autos coming and going, loud neighbors, and the like.

Security

Campground security is relative. A remote campground with no civilization nearby is relatively safe, but don't tempt potential thieves by leaving your valuables out for all to see. Use common sense, and go with your instincts. Campground hosts are wonderful to have around, and state parks with locked gates at night are ideal for security. Get to know your neighbors, and develop a buddy system to watch each other's belongings whenever possible.

Cleanliness

I'm a stickler for this one. Nothing will sabotage a scenic campground like trash. Most of the campgrounds in this book are clean. More rustic campgrounds—my favorites—usually receive less maintenance. Busy weekends and holidays will show their effects; however, don't let a little litter spoil your good time. Help clean up, and think of it as doing your part for Florida's natural environment.

:: THE CAMPGROUND PROFILE

Each profile contains a concise but informative narrative of the campground and individual sites. Not only is the property described, but readers can also get a general idea of the recreational opportunities available—what's in the area and perhaps suggestions for touristy activities. This descriptive text is enhanced with three helpful sidebars: Ratings, Key Information, and Getting There (accurate driving directions that lead you to the campground from the nearest major roadway, along with GPS coordinates).

:: THE OVERVIEW MAP, MAP KEY, AND LEGEND

Use the overview map on pages ii–iii to assess the exact location of each campground. The campground's number appears not only on the overview map but also on the map key facing the overview map, in the table of contents, and on the profile's first page. This book is organized by region, as indicated in the table of contents. A map legend that details the symbols found on the campground layout maps appears on page iv.

:: CAMPGROUND-LAYOUT MAPS

Each profile contains a detailed campground-layout map that provides an overhead look at campground sites, internal roads, facilities, and other key items.

:: GPS CAMPGROUND-ENTRANCE COORDINATES

Readers can easily access all campgrounds in this book by using the directions given and the overview map, which shows at least one major road leading into the area. But for those who enjoy using GPS technology to navigate, the book includes coordinates for each campground's entrance in latitude and longitude, expressed in degrees and decimal minutes.

To convert GPS coordinates from degrees, minutes, and seconds to the above degrees–decimal minutes format, the seconds are divided by 60. For more on GPS technology, visit usgs.gov.

About This Book

Florida is a tent camper's paradise. From the northwestern Panhandle to the Everglades, there are natural areas, still wild, that have been developed enough to include campgrounds of high quality. So you can camp in an attractive setting and have plenty of nature nearby to enjoy. And with the focus on tourism in the state, you're never more than a couple hours' drive from attractions designed for the out-of-towner.

Tent-camping opportunities vary with the change of seasons in Florida. Yes, there is a degree of seasonality in Florida, a seasonality that is more noticeable the farther north you are. Tallahassee can get downright cold in January. Also, the change of seasons north of the state line will affect your tent-camping experience south of it. In winter, snowbirds descend from Canada and the northern states, occupying the campgrounds in south and central Florida. In summer, many of these same campgrounds become deserted.

Most snowbirds travel in RVs. Usually the RVs and tents are separated; however, in some campgrounds, they are not. Some of the best campgrounds mix RVs and tent campers; these campgrounds have other qualities too good to eliminate them from this book for that reason alone. That's just the way of the camping world in some parts of Florida. Try not to let it bother you—enjoy the scenery instead.

As you move north, there are campgrounds, especially oceanside ones, which get a modicum of year-round traffic. Winter can bring a solitude that is not experienced at other times of the year at certain Panhandle campgrounds. So, when tent camping in Florida, take the time of year into account when choosing your getaway. To help with your planning, I have included in each campground description my recommendation for the best time of year to camp there.

A few words of advice: call ahead or look on the Internet for a park brochure, map, or other information to help you plan your trip. Get reservations where applicable, especially in the Keys. Ask questions. Ask more questions. The more questions you ask, the fewer surprises you'll get. There are other times, however, when you'll grab your gear and this book, hop in the car, and just wing it. This can be an adventure in its own right.

In Florida, you must plan for the probability of bugs. Mosquitoes and no-see-ums can plot to ruin a camping trip. Don't let them do it. Bring repellent, a tent with fine mesh netting, and a good attitude.

:: FIRST-AID KIT

A useful first-aid kit may contain more items than you might think necessary. These are just the basics. Prepackaged kits in waterproof bags (Atwater Carey and Adventure Medical make them) are available. As a preventive measure, take along sunscreen and insect repellent. Even though quite a few items are listed here, they pack down into a small space:

- Ace bandages or Spenco joint wraps
- Adhesive bandages, such as Band-Aids
- Antibiotic ointment *(Neosporin or the generic equivalent)*
- Antiseptic or disinfectant, such as Betadine or hydrogen peroxide
- Aspirin or acetaminophen
- Benadryl or the generic equivalent, diphenhydramine *(in case of allergic reactions)*
- Butterfly-closure bandages
- Comb and tweezers *(for removing stray cactus needles from your skin)*
- Emergency poncho
- Epinephrine in a prefilled syringe *(for people known to have severe allergic reactions to such things as bee stings)*
- Gauze *(one roll and six 4-by-4-inch pads)*
- LED flashlight or headlamp
- Matches or lighter
- Mirror for signaling passing aircraft
- Moleskin/Spenco 2nd Skin
- Pocketknife or multipurpose tool
- Waterproof first-aid tape
- Whistle *(it's more effective in signaling rescuers than your voice)*

:: CAMPING ETIQUETTE

Here are some simple tips to keep you on good terms with your camping neighbors, campground personnel, and all of us who will come camping after you.

- **Obtain all permits and authorizations required.** Make sure you check in, pay your fee, and mark your site as directed. If the sign says to check in first, but you'd like to visually scope out the sites first, just ask.

■ **Follow the campground's rules regarding building fires, facility usage,** parking, check-out times, number of people per site, and so on; ask if you need an exception. If the rule says six people per site, but your nephew makes seven, check in advance if that would be acceptable. Most campground hosts are flexible with reasonable requests.

■ **Leave only footprints.** Be sensitive to the ground beneath you. Be sure to place all garbage in designated receptacles or pack it out if none is available. If there was trash when you arrived, take care of it as well, and leave the campsite better than you found it. Never burn garbage–trash smoke smells bad, and trash debris in a fire ring is unsightly.

■ **Be courteous to other campers, hikers, bikers, and others you encounter:** Respect their privacy and space unless invited–don't hike through their site to get to yours. If there are other choices, don't set up camp next to someone who has obviously selected a secluded site. It may be the best area of the campground, but that person got there first, so you should look elsewhere. Avoid, if you can, arriving late at night and attempting to set up camp in the glare of your headlights. If you must arrive late, look for a site away from others, plan to light a lantern, unload all at once (so you don't have to keep slamming car doors), and set up quietly. Keep the noise level down in your party, even if it's not officially quiet hours. If you camp with a dog, be sure it doesn't bark at passersby or noises in the night. Keep it leashed and clean up after it. Dog waste is not the same as wild-animal waste. Those camping after you won't want to deal with it, and it can be harmful to the environment.

■ **Plan ahead.** Know your equipment, your ability, and the area in which you are camping, and prepare accordingly. Be self-sufficient at all times; carry necessary supplies for changes in weather and other conditions.

:: TIPS FOR A HAPPY CAMPING TRIP

There is nothing worse than a bad camping trip, especially because it is so easy to have a great time. To assist with making your outing a happy one, here are some pointers:

■ **Reserve your site ahead of time,** especially if it's a weekend or a holiday, or if the campground is wildly popular. Many prime campgrounds require significant lead time on reservations. Check before you go.

■ **Pick your camping buddies wisely.** A family trip is pretty straightforward, but you may want to reconsider including grumpy Uncle Fred, who doesn't like bugs, sunshine, or marshmallows. After you know who's going, make sure that everyone is on the same page regarding expectations of difficulty (amenities or the lack thereof, physical exertion, and so on), sleeping arrangements, and food requirements.

■ **Don't duplicate equipment,** such as cooking pots and lanterns, among campers in your party. Carry what you need to have a good time, but don't turn the trip into a major moving experience.

■ **Dress for the season.** Educate yourself on the temperature highs and lows of the specific area you plan to visit.

■ **Pitch your tent on a level surface,** preferably one covered with leaves, pine straw, or grass. Use a tarp or specially designed footprint to thwart ground moisture and to protect the tent floor. Do a little site maintenance, such as picking up the small rocks and sticks that can damage your tent floor and make sleep uncomfortable. If you have a separate tent rainfly but don't think you'll need it, keep it rolled up at the base of the tent in case it starts raining at midnight.

■ **If you are not comfortable sleeping on the ground,** take a sleeping pad with you that is full-length and thicker than you think you might need. This will not only keep your hips from aching on hard ground, but will also help keep you warm. A wide range of thin, light, inflatable pads is available at camping stores today, and these are a much better choice than home air mattresses, which conduct heat away from the body and tend to deflate during the night.

■ **If you're not hiking into a primitive campsite,** there is no real need to skimp on food due to weight. Plan tasty meals and bring everything you will need to prepare, cook, eat, and clean up.

■ **If you tend to use the bathroom multiple times at night, you should plan ahead.** Leaving a warm sleeping bag and stumbling around in the dark to find the restroom, whether it be a pit toilet, a fully plumbed comfort station, or just the woods, is not fun. Keep a flashlight and any other accoutrements you may need by the tent door and know exactly where to head in the dark.

■ **Standing dead trees and storm-damaged living trees can pose a real hazard to tent campers.** These trees may have loose or broken limbs that could fall at any time. When choosing a campsite or even just a spot to rest during a hike, look up.

:: CHANGES

While campgrounds are less prone to change than big-time tourist attractions, they are nevertheless subject to agency budgets, upgrades and dilapidation, and even natural disasters. With that in mind, it's a good idea to call ahead for the most updated report on the campground you've selected. We appreciate being told about any notable changes that you come across while using this book and welcome all reader input, including suggestions for potential entries for future editions. Send them to the author, in care of Menasha Ridge Press at the address provided on the copyright page.

Florida Panhandle

1

Big Lagoon State Park Campground

Big Lagoon State Park Campground was built on an ancient, wooded sand dune, which accounts for the varied campsites you find there today.

Located on the Intracoastal Water-way, Big Lagoon is Florida's most westerly recreation area. The water-dominated park has fishing, boating, hiking, swimming, and camping. Nearby Perdido Key Recreation Area features a white-sand Gulf beach. Big Lagoon's campground has a mix of sites to suit any camper's desires. Look over the campground before you pick a site, or you'll miss out on a campsite that you wish you could have had.

Big Lagoon Campground was built on an ancient, wooded sand dune, which accounts for the varied campsites you find there today. A very long and narrow

:: Ratings

BEAUTY: ★ ★ ★ ★
PRIVACY: ★ ★ ★ ★
SPACIOUSNESS: ★ ★ ★ ★
QUIET: ★ ★ ★
SECURITY: ★ ★ ★ ★ ★
CLEANLINESS: ★ ★ ★ ★

loop road runs along either low side of the dune. This setup makes for a rolling campground with vertical relief, unusual for Florida. Differing degrees of forest cover make for both sunny, open campsites and hidden, wooded campsites.

Tall slash pines tower above the campground, but the more prevalent pine is the low-slung sand pine that favors sandy coastal regions like Big Lagoon. Live oaks grow about, but they don't reach the heights seen farther inland. Plants like dune rosemary combine with wax myrtle, winged sumac, and palmetto to form thick campsite buffers that shield you from your neighbor.

Enter the loop. The campsites on the right-hand side of the loop are higher and have less-dense woodlands. The other side of the loop backs against a marsh and has campsites cut into moist woods. Still other sites are cut into the dune and have wooden walls to hold back the sand.

The sites in the back of the camp-ground are better suited for tent camp-ers. Quaint wooden fences separate some

:: Key Information

ADDRESS: Big Lagoon State Park
12301 Gulf Beach Highway
Pensacola, FL 32507

OPERATED BY: Florida State Parks

CONTACT: 850-492-1595, floridastate
parks.org; reservations 800-326-3521,
reserveamerica.com

OPEN: Year-round

SITES: 75

EACH SITE: Picnic table, fire ring,
water, electricity

ASSIGNMENT: Self-assignment via
Reserve America, otherwise assigned
by ranger

REGISTRATION: By phone, online, or
at park entrance booth

FACILITIES: Hot showers, flush toilets,
dump station

PARKING: At campsites only in
campground

FEE: $20/night

ELEVATION: Sea level

RESTRICTIONS:

■ **Pets:** On 6-foot leash; proof of
vaccination required

■ **Fires:** In fire rings only

■ **Alcohol:** Prohibited

■ **Vehicles:** None

■ **Other:** 14-day stay limit

of the campsites and protect fragile buffer vegetation. This area is the highest in the campground and has many appealing sites: adequate space and privacy can be found at nearly every one.

Three clean and modern comfort stations serve the campground. Campground hosts and on-site rangers make this a very safe place to camp.

Park recreation is just a walk away. Two nature trails leave the campground via boardwalks and connect to the waters of the Intracoastal Waterway. There are two swimming areas: East Beach and West Beach. Neat, wooden picnic pavilions offer refuge from the sun between playtime in the water. East Beach has an observation tower overlooking the surrounding Gulf beaches and waters.

Quality saltwater fishing for sea trout and flounder is available. Boaters have a boat ramp to launch their craft. Hungry campers can even go crabbing in Big Lagoon.

All these nature trails connect to make nearly all park areas accessible. The Yaupon Trail meanders right along the Intracoastal Waterway. The Grand Lagoon Trail connects East Beach to West Beach and has a side trail to Big Lagoon itself. The 3.5-mile Cookie Trail is a one-way trek that starts near the park entrance station. It passes through open pine woods and nearly impenetrable thickets gnarled from the salt and wind of the maritime weather.

It is about a 15-minute drive to Perdido Key from Big Lagoon. Perdido Key State Park is a 247-acre enclave of

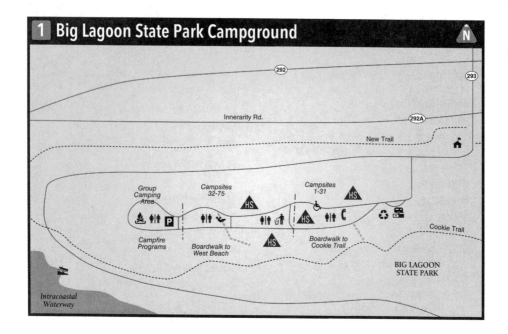

1 Big Lagoon State Park Campground

protected Gulf coast. There are more than 1.4 miles of beach to enjoy. Clear waters meld into white-sand beaches, which become rolling sand dunes covered with sea oats. Several boardwalks crisscross the environment, making for safe passage across the fragile sand dunes. To access Perdido Key, turn left out of Big Lagoon

and then take your next left onto FL 292; follow it a short distance to the state park.

Big Lagoon was a pleasant surprise for me. I really enjoyed the unusual campground stretched along the ancient sand dune. The park recreation and that of nearby Perdido Key offer any tent camper ample reason to give Big Lagoon a try.

:: Getting There

From Pensacola, take US 98 West from Navy Boulevard 6 miles to County Road 293 (Bauer Road). Turn left on CR 293 and head south 5 miles to dead-end at Big Lagoon State Park.

GPS COORDINATES   N30° 19' 15.2"   W87° 24' 13.2"

2

Blackwater River State Park Campground

This water-oriented park has a fine campground.
It's a pleasant stay even if you are not a paddler.

The **Blackwater River** enjoys a reputation as the cleanest river in the state of Florida. Most of its upper drainage flows through protected forestlands. The clear waters have a reddish tint from tree tannin. The river bottom is sugar-white sand. This sand builds to form sandbars on river bends. These sandbars make great swimming, picnicking, and overnight camping spots for river runners. Most paddlers end their trips at Blackwater River State Park, which makes it a great base camp to paddle not only the Blackwater but also three other fantastic waters nearby: Sweetwater, Juniper, and Coldwater Creeks. Many outfitters serve the locality, which makes an outing convenient and easy, whether or not you have your own canoe.

:: Ratings

BEAUTY: ★ ★ ★ ★
PRIVACY: ★ ★ ★
SPACIOUSNESS: ★ ★ ★
QUIET: ★ ★ ★ ★
SECURITY: ★ ★ ★ ★ ★
CLEANLINESS: ★ ★ ★ ★

The campground is scenic in its own right. Heavily wooded, with a dense growth of campsite buffers, the camping area is split into two loops. The heady aroma of longleaf pine, the area's predominant tree, filters through the campground. Oak, maple, and a few hardwoods are scattered about. The close proximity to the Blackwater brings some riverine flora to the area.

The right-hand loop has 15 campsites. Dense vegetation forms ideal campsite buffers for tent campers. This is the shadier of the two loops and is closer to the river. The campsites are smaller here than on the other loop, yet have adequate space. Generally, a little sacrificed space is the price you pay for increased privacy. The left-hand loop has 15 campsites as well. Having two loops disperses campers and increases the sense of serenity here at Blackwater. The campsites here are bigger and more open than those on the right-hand loop. Their larger size attracts some RVs to this particular loop. The facilities are well maintained and attract campers year after year. The paddling season on the Blackwater heats up in May and lasts

:: Key Information

ADDRESS: Blackwater River State Park
7720 Deaton Bridge Road
Holt, FL 32564

OPERATED BY: Florida State Parks

CONTACT: 850-983-5363, floridastate
parks.org; reservations 800-326-3521,
reserveamerica.com

OPEN: Year-round

SITES: 30

EACH SITE: Picnic table, fire ring,
water, electricity, sewer

ASSIGNMENT: First come, first served;
self-assignment via Reserve America

REGISTRATION: At ranger station

FACILITIES: Hot showers, flush toilets

PARKING: At campsites only;
overnight parking for paddling trips

FEE: $20/night

ELEVATION: 30'

RESTRICTIONS:

■ **Pets:** On 6-foot leash only

■ **Fires:** In fire rings only

■ **Alcohol:** In designated areas only

■ **Vehicles:** None

■ **Other:** 14-day stay limit

through September. However, I've enjoyed the river in all seasons and recommend the same for you. This is when the campground gets busy too. The cooler months are very quiet, except for travelers looking for an overnight stopping place. An early weekend arrival will most likely land a pleasant campsite.

You don't have to paddle the Blackwater to enjoy the cool water and white sand. A boardwalk leads from the river parking area to covered picnic shelters and the river. Here you can sunbathe and swim. Check out the Florida-record-size Atlantic white cedar tree along the boardwalk.

Hikers have two trails on which to stretch their legs. A short nature trail leaves the campground and leads to the river. The trail loops a small pond that was once the source of the shallow Blackwater. On the other side of the river is the 1-mile Chain of Lakes Trail, known for its birding

opportunities. The path follows the river and then meanders through low-lying cypress swamps and small lakes.

But the main activity at Blackwater is paddling. Several outfitters in the area will be glad to serve you. On my trips down local rivers, I have used Adventures Unlimited, adventuresunlimited.com. The number is 850-623-6197. The staff will rent kayaks and canoes or provide shuttle service for those who bring their own watercraft.

Why paddle the Blackwater? Cedar trees lining the riverbanks. Cypress, oak, and maple trees swaying in the breeze. Pine trees on the higher ground. Swift-moving waters sweeping around bends, passing huge, white sandbars that beckon you to wiggle your toes in the sand. The relaxation of just floating down the river. A riverbank picnic. Sun on your face. Clean, natural water that you feel comfortable swimming in.

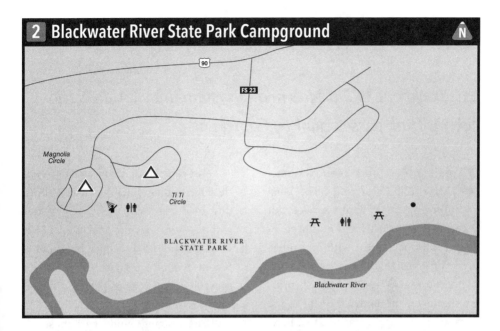

2 Blackwater River State Park Campground

Magnolia Circle

Ti Ti Circle

BLACKWATER RIVER STATE PARK

Blackwater River

Other smaller streams in the area exhibit these same qualities. I like Coldwater Creek. It is small, shallow, and fast—supposedly the fastest water in the area. Fallen trees on bends keep canoeists on their toes. Ample sandbars allow for frequent stops.

You can paddle two creeks on the Sweetwater–Juniper run. These are even smaller than Coldwater. Start on the Sweetwater to its confluence with the Juniper and keep floating down the Juniper. Other runs that are solely on the Juniper are rewarding too. Keep an eye downriver, as logs and submerged obstructions can come up quickly on these swift streams.

This water-oriented park has a fine campground. It's a pleasant stay even if you are not a paddler. The park section of the Blackwater is accessible for foot travelers. So, one way or another, get in the water at Blackwater River State Park.

:: Getting There

From Milton, drive east on US 90 for 11 miles to the tiny town of Harold. Turn left on Forest Route 23, which will have a sign indicating it is the route to Blackwater River State Park. Follow FR 23 for 3 miles to Blackwater River State Park.

GPS COORDINATES   N30° 42' 34.3" W86° 52' 45.3"

3

Camel Lake Campground

The backbone of Florida's hiking system, the Florida National Scenic Trail, passes right by Camel Lake.

Small, quiet, and scenic. Camel Lake Campground has been revamped by the US Forest Service, but its natural beauty needed no improvements: an open forest with an understory of grass that turns to brooding cypress trees covered in Spanish moss by the lake. The body of water is the focal point of the recreation area. Bicyclers and hikers will be glad to know that the Florida National Scenic Trail and a few other paths make overland recreation possible too.

As it stands, there are 10 campsites. Half have been electrified, but half remain primitive. The figure may change again with time, but the overall number of campsites will remain small. It couldn't be any other way at this off-the-beaten-path campground.

:: Ratings

> BEAUTY: ★ ★ ★
> PRIVACY: ★ ★
> SPACIOUSNESS: ★ ★ ★ ★ ★
> QUIET: ★ ★ ★ ★
> SECURITY: ★ ★ ★
> CLEANLINESS: ★ ★ ★ ★

The campground is located on a gentle slope leading to Camel Lake. A short, dirt road connects the camping area with the paved day-use area. Camel Lake Campground is mostly open but is punctuated by pine trees and turkey oaks. A sporadic understory of palmetto breaks up the camping area.

The campground bathhouse is about 50 yards away from the campsites in the day-use area. It has flush toilets for each sex. This area used to be part of the campground. A grassy lawn overlooks the lake and is backed by a denser forest than the campground. A cold-water shower is out in the open in the day-use area; wear your trunks or swimsuit if you shower here.

Spring-fed Camel Lake attracts anglers from all around. Big bass have been pulled out of these waters. Bream and catfish are here too. Launch your boat at the nearby boat ramp. Directly below the day-use area is a large, grassy lawn that leads down to a swimming beach. The swimming area is ringed off for children's safety.

The backbone of Florida's hiking system, the Florida National Scenic Trail,

:: Key Information

ADDRESS: Camel Lake Campground 11152 NW FL 20, Bristol, FL 32321

OPERATED BY: US Forest Service

CONTACT: 850-643-2282, www.fs.usda.gov/apalachicola

OPEN: Year-round

SITES: 5 electric, 5 nonelectric

EACH SITE: Picnic table, fire ring, grill, lantern post

ASSIGNMENT: First come, first served; no reservations

REGISTRATION: Self-registration on-site

FACILITIES: Flush toilets, water spigots

PARKING: At campsites only

FEE: $10 per night nonelectric, $15 electric

ELEVATION: 55'

RESTRICTIONS:

■ **Pets:** On 6-foot leash maximum

■ **Fires:** In fire rings only

■ **Alcohol:** Prohibited

■ **Vehicles:** None

■ **Other:** 14-day stay limit

passes right by Camel Lake. Follow the blue blazes on the trees from the recreation area entrance and go a few hundred feet to intersect the orange-blazed trail. You can go either north or south on this trail. The southern route travels through varied environments from dry, sandhill country to junglelike areas near streams. The northern route swings by Memery Island to end at FL 12. Arrange for a shuttle to pick you up.

The Camel Lake Loop Trail starts at the boat launch. The numbered footpath circles Camel Lake and smaller Camel Pond. If you follow the numbers in their entirety, the loop trip is 1.8 miles. If you bypass Camel Pond and only circle Camel Lake, the trip is 1.2 miles. Camel Pond has a few fish in it too. The Camel Lake Interpretive Trail starts across the road from the campground entrance. Signs tell you all about this Florida Panhandle forest on the 1-mile loop.

A campground host mans the front gate, making for a safer campground. The day-use area at Camel Lake can be busy on summer weekends, but with only 10 campsites, the campground can't get too crowded. Set up your tent and get to know your fellow campers.

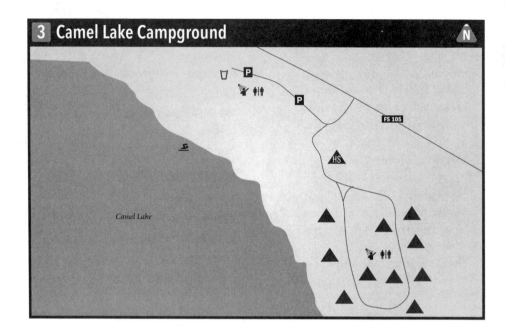

:: Getting There

From Bristol, take Country Road 12 south about 11 miles. Turn left on Forest Route 105 and drive 2 miles. Camel Lake Campground will be on your right.

GPS COORDINATES   N30° 16′ 36.74″   W84° 59′ 16.81″

4

Dead Lakes Park Campground

*The solitude you find here happens to be
Dead Lakes' greatest asset.*

Upon arriving at Dead Lakes Park, I looked around for a park ranger. Finally I gave up, set up camp, and set about having a good time. The birds were my only companions, serenading me, unseen in the distance. Other than the birds, Dead Lakes is very quiet. It's not that the place is unappealing—it's just near enough to the beach that most campers pass it by. The name doesn't exactly draw you in either. But the solitude you find here happens to be Dead Lakes' greatest asset.

Weeks go by and very few people overnight in the campground. This small park—83 acres—sees its fair share of day visitors. They are mostly locals doing a little fishing in the Dead Lakes. Granted, this isn't a place to spend two weeks, but the park makes an ideal overnighting

:: Ratings

BEAUTY: ★ ★ ★
PRIVACY: ★ ★ ★ ★ ★
SPACIOUSNESS: ★ ★ ★ ★
QUIET: ★ ★ ★ ★ ★
SECURITY: ★ ★ ★ ★
CLEANLINESS: ★ ★ ★ ★

place on the way to the Gulf beaches or a place where you can have the whole campground to yourself. No hustle and bustle here. None whatsoever.

The small campground is located under a stand of tall longleaf pines. An old sand road makes a loop through the woods. At the beginning of the loop are three campsites that have the most bushes in the campground, but campsite privacy is irrelevant here. Chances are you'll have the entire campground to yourself. The understory of grass and pinecones in the campsite parking spots stands testimony to the limited use of this little-known campground.

Beyond the 3 sites is the beginning of 10 campsites located on the inside of the loop, with more sand than grass for an understory. You'll also be closer to the immaculate comfort station in the loop's center. It has hot showers and flush toilets and is guaranteed to be unoccupied.

As the loop continues, other large sites sit on the loop's exterior, on the highest land in the campground. These sites are fine as well. Just take your time; nobody will be driving up to steal your coveted campsite. I've been told by the

:: Key Information

<table>
<tr><td>

ADDRESS: Dead Lakes Park
P.O. Box 667, 318 South Seventh St.
Wewahitchka, FL 32465

OPERATED BY: Gulf County

CONTACT: 850-639-2238

OPEN: Year-round

SITES: 25

EACH SITE: Picnic table, fire ring, grill, water, electricity

ASSIGNMENT: First come, first served; no reservations

REGISTRATION: Ranger will come by and register you

</td><td>

FACILITIES: Hot showers, flush toilets, water spigots

PARKING: At campsites only

FEE: $14/night nonelectric; $18 with electricity

ELEVATION: 40′

RESTRICTIONS:

■ **Pets:** On leash only

■ **Fires:** In fire rings only

■ **Alcohol:** Prohibited

■ **Vehicles:** None

■ **Other:** None

</td></tr>
</table>

powers that be the campground has never been filled to capacity.

If you've been driving a bit, there is about a mile's worth of nature trails to walk and stretch your legs. They start right near the campground and pass by some old ponds that were once used to hold fish for a nearby hatchery.

Of course, the primary waters are the Dead Lakes themselves, which is really one lake. Dead Lakes—what a name! This place came to be when sandbars formed where the Chipola River entered the Apalachicola River. This backed up the water and flooded the Chipola, creating five wide spots in the river. This flooding killed a vast number of trees in the new lake, which thereafter became known as the Dead Lakes.

Mankind meddled with the relationship between the Chipola and Apalachicola, but today things are fine with the lake. Dead Lakes offers some seriously good bass fishing. A boat ramp is located at the park. There is also a fishing pier for the boatless. You can use a canoe, kayak, or powerboat to angle for bream and crappie, as well as bass. A quality paddling run on the Chipola ends at the Dead Lakes. The Apalachicola makes for a fine paddling adventure, too, especially if you like big, moving water.

I enjoyed my visit to the park. A warm wind blew through the spring day as I ate lunch in the picnic area near the campground. The campground was my own. Actually, the whole park was my own. It was a bit warm walking the nature trails, but the wind was too strong to paddle the lake.

When you come to Dead Lakes, expect few other campers for company.

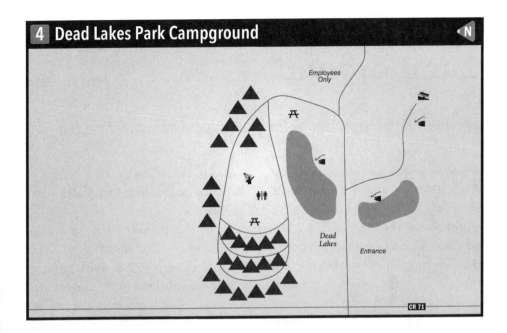

4 Dead Lakes Park Campground

Bring in all your own supplies, entertainment, and friends. And while you are in the area, stop to appreciate the peace and quiet in this slice of the Panhandle.

:: Getting There

From Wewahitchka, drive north on FL 71 for 2 miles. Turn right into Dead Lakes Park.

GPS COORDINATES   N30° 8' 29.1" W85° 12' 1.9"

5

Falling Waters State Park Campground

The hilltop campground is long on appeal and short on crowds.

was surprised upon seeing this 155-acre state park. The small size had me wondering just how good it could be. It was better than expected. Granted, the dimensions limit how much you can do and how long you will want to stay, but if you have a night and are in the area, don't pass it by. The hilltop campground is long on appeal and short on crowds. The natural features of the park are worth an afternoon of your time.

The Pine Ridge Camping Area sits at the park's high point. It's 250 feet in elevation—lofty country by Florida standards and the highest campground in this entire guide. Top the hill and enter a grove of longleaf and slash pine. The U-shaped campground road slowly curves to the left and descends a mild slope. Vertical relief in Florida campgrounds is unusual and adds to the scenic beauty of this particular site.

Four of the first five campsites are pull-through. This spells RV; but don't worry, there probably won't be more than one RV in the entire campground. Actually, you'll be hard pressed for neighbors, whether they be tent campers or RVers. The ranger told me Falling Waters averaged two or three campers per night at the 24-unit campground. It fills up two weekends per year: Memorial Day and Labor Day.

Beyond the pull-through sites starts a string of 10 campsites; these are the park's best. Between tall pines are stretches of grass strewn with pine needles and peppered with pinecones. A few bushes break up the area. It just has the look that makes you want to run through it. These prime campsites are on both sides of the paved road.

Pass a couple of sites at the low point of the campground, and the road starts to climb again. Here are two more pull-through sites. Three additional pull-in sites at the back of a small turnaround are very appealing.

:: Ratings

BEAUTY: ★ ★ ★ ★
PRIVACY: ★ ★ ★
SPACIOUSNESS: ★ ★ ★ ★ ★
QUIET: ★ ★ ★ ★
SECURITY: ★ ★ ★ ★ ★
CLEANLINESS: ★ ★ ★ ★ ★

:: Key Information

ADDRESS: Falling Waters State Park 1130 State Park Road Chipley, FL 32428	**REGISTRATION:** At ranger station
	FACILITIES: Showers, flush toilets
OPERATED BY: Florida State Parks	**PARKING:** At campsites only
	FEE: $18/per night
CONTACT: 850-638-6130, floridastate parks.org; reservations 800-326-3521, reserveamerica.com	**ELEVATION:** 250'
	RESTRICTIONS:
OPEN: Year-round	■ **Pets:** On leash and attended at all times
SITES: 24	
EACH SITE: Picnic table, fire ring, water, electricity	■ **Fires:** In fire rings only
	■ **Alcohol:** Prohibited
ASSIGNMENT: First come, first served; and by reservation	■ **Vehicles:** None
	■ **Other:** None

There are a few wax myrtles, dog-woods, and turkey oaks about the campground; however, they provide little in the way of campsite privacy. Yet here at Falling Waters, privacy is a nonissue because you will most likely be camping 100 feet or more from any other campers. And speaking of room, the campsites offer the maximum in site spaciousness.

The main attraction of the park is also an unusual Florida feature—a waterfall. The Falling Water Sink is a designated Florida Natural Feature. Though this area has hills, to get a 73-foot falls requires a hole—a sinkhole. The waterfall is created by a small creek flowing into a cylindrical hole. Take the Sinks Trail to the waterfall. As you descend the walkway to the falls, the air around you cools significantly. The waterfall truly is attractive.

Two other interesting nature trails spur off the Sinks Trail. The Wiregrass Trail passes through pine woodland past an old oil-well drill site. This was one of the first oil-drilling locations in the Sunshine State. This area also saw a gristmill and even a little moonshining back in the olden days.

The Sinkhole Trail rides a boardwalk up, down, and around more sinkholes of varying sizes and depths. It's a good thing this trail has a handrail—previous hikers have probably fallen in. The Terrace Trail runs from the campground through an old pine plantation—watch for the rows of trees. This area was also the site of a plant nursery in the early 1900s. The trail ends at a two-acre lake with a roped-off swimming area and a small beach.

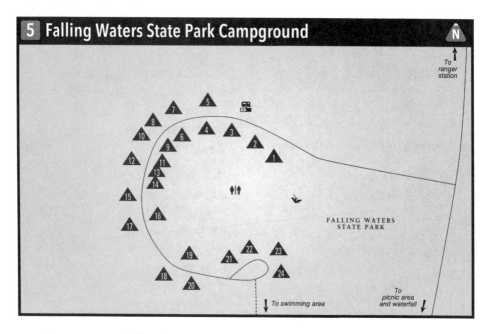

As you can see, Falling Waters State Park makes the most of its 155 acres. The land is rural nearby, resulting in a peaceful setting that makes for a great one-night stopover in a pretty little campground.

:: Getting There

From Chipley, take FL 77 south 4 miles to State Park Road. Turn left on State Park Road and follow it 1 mile. Falling Waters State Park will be dead ahead.

GPS COORDINATES   N30° 43' 32.4"   W85° 31' 39.5"

6

Florida Caverns State Park Campground

Florida Caverns State Park offers aboveground, belowground, and water recreation.

The name of this state park emphasizes the uniqueness of the underground features here. Strange and fascinating rock formations characterize the cave, where a tour guide leads you safely past the many sights to see. There are also many aboveground reasons to come to Florida Caverns, including the Chipola River and the fine campground.

Camping here is an eye-pleasing experience in the diversely wooded setting. Laurel oaks and pines form the nucleus of the trees, but smaller beech, southern magnolia, and dogwood make for a varied setting in which to pitch your tent. Trees and bushes allow for plenty of site privacy and create the impression that the campground was integrated into the forest rather than the other way around.

:: Ratings

BEAUTY: ★ ★ ★ ★
PRIVACY: ★ ★ ★
SPACIOUSNESS: ★ ★ ★ ★
QUIET: ★ ★ ★
SECURITY: ★ ★ ★ ★ ★
CLEANLINESS: ★ ★ ★ ★

Blue Hole Camping Area is formed by a large, oval loop. The campground is split into four distinct sections, each containing several campsites. A low-lying cypress swamp and Carters Mill Branch nearly encircle the campground with water, but the camping area is high and dry.

Half the sites are on the inside of the loop. Generally, the larger sites are on the outside of the loop, where I personally prefer to camp. But all the campsites are roomy; some are just extra roomy. Having the campsites spaced in four different sections along the loop provides everyone with plenty of personal room. Three tent-only campsites are tucked away on their own.

If you can find it in the dense forest, the center of the loop holds a large bathhouse with all the expected amenities of a state park. This campground can fill up on summer and holiday weekends. Fall is an excellent time to come—the deciduous hardwoods can put on quite a colorful show throughout the park. It is fairly quiet during the winter. Spring sees many paddlers floating the Chipola.

:: Key Information

ADDRESS: Florida Caverns State Park 3345 Caverns Road Marianna, FL 32446	**REGISTRATION:** By phone or at the ranger station
	FACILITIES: Showers, flush toilets
OPERATED BY: Florida State Parks	**PARKING:** At campsites only
CONTACT: 850-482-1228, floridastateparks.org; reservations 800-326-3521, reserveamerica.com	**FEE:** $20/per night
	ELEVATION: 120'
OPEN: Year-round	**RESTRICTIONS:**
SITES: 35	■ **Pets:** On 6-foot leash
EACH SITE: Picnic table, fire ring, water, electricity	■ **Fires:** In fire rings only
	■ **Alcohol:** Prohibited
ASSIGNMENT: Assigned by ranger	■ **Vehicles:** None
	■ **Other:** 14-day stay limit

No matter the weather or the season, Florida Caverns is ready to be toured. These tours are offered daily. Just drive to the visitor center and wait for the next tour to begin. They last 45 minutes and can be had for a reasonable fee. From the roof of the cave, stalactites descend to meet the stalagmites pyramiding from the floor, ever rising from the minerals dripping from the ceiling above.

As you look at the impressive formations, be aware that they are being formed at the nearly imperceptible rate of one cubic inch per hundred years. Some of the pathways are a tight squeeze, but this makes the tour fun. The cave ranges from 62°F to 68°F year-round. I give the tour a hearty recommendation.

Before or after you tour the cave, I also suggest walking the nature trails that depart from the visitor center parking area. The Floodplain Trail passes a couple of caves of its own. The trail looks out over the Chipola River. Indians once lived here; you can see a small shelter once used as living quarters. The Beech-Magnolia Trail connects with the Floodplain Trail, and they all add up to more than a mile of informative walking.

The Blue Hole lies near the campground. It is a spring that has been developed into a swimming area. A nice, grassy lawn is ideal for sunbathing, and a roped-off swimming spot will keep you cool. A short path connects the campground to the Blue Hole.

Anglers and paddlers will want to utilize the Chipola River. It makes a good float. In the park, the river once sank into the ground, then rose several hundred feet away; loggers have cut a channel reconnecting the river. Canoes can be rented at the park. Outfitters based in the area will rent kayaks and canoes in

6 Florida Caverns State Park Campground

Equestrian Facility

33 34 35

Blue Hole Drive

Blue Hole swimming area

To 166

FLORIDA CAVERNS STATE PARK

Chipola River

Path

Sites 1-8

Sites 25-32

Sites 9-16

Blue Hole Campground

Sites 17-24

addition to providing shuttle service for a trip. Visit the park office for information.

The Blue Hole Campground is a relaxing setting. Florida Caverns State Park offers aboveground, belowground, and water recreation. Come on by and give it a chance.

:: Getting There

From downtown Marianna, take County Road 166 (Jefferson Street) 3 miles north. Florida Caverns State Park will be on your left.

GPS COORDINATES   N30° 48′ 49.1″ 85° 12′ 27.8″

7

Grayton Beach State Park Campground

If you like to relax on the beach and come back to a soothing, private campground, this is the place for you.

Simply put, if you are in the area, don't pass by Grayton Beach State Park. The campground is heavily vegetated in native flora and is just the right size. The addition of a camping loop with larger sites has had the effect of segregating RVs and tent campers. Grayton Beach itself is as fine as the grains of white sand from which it is made. If you like to relax on the beach and come back to a soothing, private campground, this is the place for you.

Though the campground is not directly on the beach, it is close enough to hear the surf crashing against the shoreline. Between the ocean and the campground is a thin strip of land and Western Lake. Western Lake is a body of water with

:: Ratings

BEAUTY: ★ ★ ★ ★ ★
PRIVACY: ★ ★ ★ ★ ★
SPACIOUSNESS: ★ ★ ★
QUIET: ★ ★ ★ ★
SECURITY: ★ ★ ★ ★ ★
CLEANLINESS: ★ ★ ★ ★

a moderate sand beach of its own that pales in scenery only when compared with one of the best beaches in the country.

The loop road design is the only standard thing about the older loop of the campground. A crushed-shell road passes through a thick wood. Overhead is a scattering of slash pines. The forest is mostly low, the result of the effects of salt spray and wind. Scrub oaks are blown into twisted shapes amid dense thickets of yaupon holly and palmetto. A few palm trees and cedars complete the vegetative picture.

This low-slung woodland is so thick that campers can hardly see their neighbors. This campground ranks with the highest in campsite privacy. The disadvantage of the low forest is a lack of shade during the high-sun hours. But that won't matter because you will probably be at the beach anyway during that time.

The Florida park service has added a second loop to the campground. It offers large sites along a paved road. Large concrete pads and sewer attract the RVs. In fact, the campground was built to

:: Key Information

ADDRESS: Grayton Beach State Park
357 Main Park Road
Santa Rosa Beach, FL 32459

OPERATED BY: Florida State Parks

CONTACT: 850-231-4210, floridastate
parks.org; reservations 800-326-3521,
reserveamerica.com

OPEN: Year-round

SITES: 59

EACH SITE: Picnic table, fire ring,
water, electricity, sewer on some sites

ASSIGNMENT: First come, first served;
and by reservation

REGISTRATION: At park entrance
booth

FACILITIES: Showers, flush toilets

PARKING: At campsites; additional
vehicles may park at day-use parking
lot

FEE: $24/night older camping area,
$30/night newer camping area

ELEVATION: Sea level

RESTRICTIONS:

■ **Pets:** Prohibited

■ **Fires:** In fire rings only

■ **Alcohol:** Prohibited

■ **Vehicles:** None

■ **Other:** 14-day stay limit

accommodate today's monster RVs that are truly houses on wheels. This newer loop is centered with a fine bathhouse, but I'd rather stay in the old loop.

This campground continues to grow in popularity as is evidenced by the addition of the new camping loop; reservations are highly recommended.

This relatively small park has a mile of world-class beach. Translucent, green waters meet sheer, white sand backed by tall sand dunes covered in sea oats. This is the primary attraction at this state recreation area.

Being a nature trail fan, I walked the one here. It makes two loops. Odd sights on the trail are the tiny Southern magnolias that merely reach bush size because of the ever-present wind and salt. The trail climbs dunes and parallels the shores of Western Lake. The nature trail then enters the pine flatwoods before returning to the beach. The foggy day made my beach walk seem even more mystical.

A boat ramp allows access to Western Lake. Anglers can cast for both freshwater and saltwater species. Some people like to surf-fish from the shore. Canoes are available for rent at a very reasonable rate; use them only on Western Lake.

But the main activity at Grayton Beach is relaxing. Take in some of that salt air and hang out on the beach. This is one place where you don't have to compromise your camping experience for the natural experience nearby.

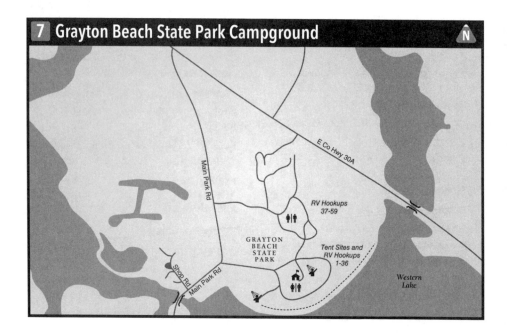

:: Getting There

From Fort Walton Beach, drive east on US 98 for 18 miles to County Road 30A. Head east on CR 30A for 9 miles. Grayton Beach State Recreation Area will be on your right.

GPS COORDINATES   N30° 19′ 29.8″ W86° 9′ 13.9″

8

High Bluff Campground

This campground near Tallahassee overlooks scenic Lake Talquin.

The **Ochlockonee River** flows out of Georgia, then becomes dammed as Lake Talquin as it enters the Sunshine State. Much of Lake Talquin's shoreline is preserved as Lake Talquin State Forest, which offers not only camping but also fishing, hiking, and mountain biking. True to its name, the campground is located on a commanding bluff rising a good 90 feet above Lake Talquin. Pines rise highest overhead, but you will probably notice the live oaks draped in Spanish moss and resurrection ferns that sway in the lake breeze.

As you enter the campground road, sites 1–10 are situated along the outside of the loop. Each site is attractive enough, though the shortcoming of the campground is evident—the campsites are simply closer together than your average

tent camper desires. However, before you quit reading, be apprised that this is less of a problem than you might think. It is very rare to have all 32 campsites filled. Therefore, campers generally take it upon themselves to spread apart, giving each site its privacy. Most of these sites are shaded, level, and attractive. As you swing around the loop, you'll find lake-view sites 8–10 before coming to the spur road and parking area near the campground fishing dock, which extends toward the water at the base of the wooded bluff. Ahead, several sites are designated tent only, though tent campers constitute the vast majority of campers here, as there is no electricity to attract RVers. Of special note is site 16, which is set under the widespread stands of live oak and is situated closest to the fishing dock. Seven more sites are on the side of the loop that offers a lake view and are thus more popular. The rest of the sites are located under shady pines, sweet gums, and laurel oaks and are fine individually, but again can be too close together. You can't lose at any site here, as the setting is quite attractive.

A T-shaped fishing dock extends well into the water and offers campers angling

:: Ratings

BEAUTY: ★ ★ ★ ★
PRIVACY: ★ ★
SPACIOUSNESS: ★ ★
QUIET: ★ ★ ★ ★
SECURITY: ★ ★ ★
CLEANLINESS: ★ ★ ★

:: Key Information

ADDRESS: Lake Talquin State Forest
865 Geddie Road
Tallahassee, FL 32304

OPERATED BY: Florida Division
of Forestry

CONTACT: 850-488-1871;
freshfromflorida.com/Divisions-
Offices/Florida-Forest-Service/Our-
Forests/State-Forests/Lake-Talquin-
State-Forest

OPEN: Year-round

SITES: 32

EACH SITE: Picnic table, fire grate

ASSIGNMENT: First come, first served;
no reservations

REGISTRATION: Self-registration

FACILITIES: Vault toilet

PARKING: At campsites only

FEE: $15/night

ELEVATION: 85'

RESTRICTIONS:

■ **Pets:** On leash only

■ **Fires:** In fire grates only

■ **Alcohol:** Prohibited

■ **Vehicles:** None

■ **Other:** 14-day stay limit in a 30-day
period

opportunities even if they are boatless. If you do have a boat, canoe, or kayak, a launch is conveniently located within walking distance of the campground. A small picnic area is also situated here. The dark waters of Lake Talquin are rimmed in cypress with evergreens rising from the hilly shores.

Trails aplenty lace the state forest, but you must drive from High Bluff to reach them. Download and print a map of the state forest before you leave home. The Fort Braden trails, on the south side of the lake, feature three loops totaling 9 miles. The Lines Tract trails add up to 10 miles and are suited for mountain bikers. The Bear Creek Tract is closest to the campground and offers 5 miles of hiker-only paths. So get your tent and your equipment and get ready for a multipronged Lake Talquin State Forest adventure.

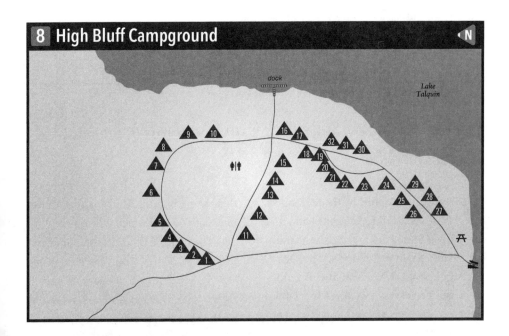

:: Getting There

From Exit 192 on I-10 west of Tallahasee, drive north on US 90 for 2.4 miles. Turn left on County Road 268/Martin Luther King Jr. Boulevard and follow it 2.5 miles to Peters Road. Turn left on Peters Road and follow it 0.9 mile. Here, the pavement ends and the road becomes High Bluff Landing Road. At 1.1 miles, veer left at the fork onto High Bluff Landing Road to reach the campground after 2.6 miles.

GPS COORDINATES   N30° 27' 40.4" W84° 29' 51.1"

9

Ochlockonee River State Park Campground

Ochlockonee River State Park is an island within an island of the real Florida.

Virtually encircled by the St. Marks National Wildlife Refuge, Ochlockonee River State Park is an island within an island of the real Florida. The Ochlockonee River is brackish at this point because it's just a few miles from the ocean. The quiet campground is a great refuge for humans.

The loop road enters the 30-site campground. Scrub live oak trees grow beneath stunted arms of longleaf pine, which stand guard over the campground. Smaller oak trees, palmetto, and other brush separate the campsites from one another. The canopy is open in spots, allowing for an airy and bright campground, yet still providing enough shade for every campsite. The landscaping in

:: Ratings

BEAUTY: ★ ★ ★ ★
PRIVACY: ★ ★ ★
SPACIOUSNESS: ★ ★ ★
QUIET: ★ ★ ★ ★ ★
SECURITY: ★ ★ ★ ★ ★
CLEANLINESS: ★ ★ ★ ★ ★

this campground is nearly perfect for the pine flatwoods in which it lies.

The first five campsites spur off from both sides of the loop. The next three sites jut out from a small parking area of their own and are more private and roomier than the first five sites.

Next begins a stretch of oak-shaded sites. Again, as the loop begins to circle back around, there are three more sites with their own parking area. One path leads to the sites. The sites have an obscured view of the Ochlockonee River and offer the most privacy in the campground. These are the most desirable sites at this park, though nearly all the sites here are good.

A bathhouse stands on the east side of the loop. This campground is small enough to be reasonably accessible for all campers. The very center of the loop is grassy and has a play area for children.

Don't blink your eyes if you see white squirrels in the campground. There is a white subspecies of squirrel living in this park. There are a few other things here you might like to see too, namely

:: Key Information

ADDRESS: Ochlockonee River State Park, 429 State Park Road Sopchoppy, FL 32358

OPERATED BY: Florida Park Services

CONTACT: 850-962-2771, floridastate parks.org; reservations 800-326-3521, reserveamerica.com

OPEN: Year-round

SITES: 30 electric

EACH SITE: Picnic table, fire ring, water spigot, electricity

ASSIGNMENT: First come, first served; or at reserveamerica.com

REGISTRATION: Ranger will come by and register you

FACILITIES: Showers, flush toilets

PARKING: At campsites only

FEE: $18/night

ELEVATION: 5'

RESTRICTIONS:

■ **Pets:** On maximum 6-foot leash

■ **Fires:** In fire rings only

■ **Alcohol:** Prohibited

■ **Vehicles:** None

the water features. This park is practically encircled by the Dead River and the Ochlockonee River, both of which can be accessed by motorboat or self-propelled craft. Both rivers offer freshwater and saltwater fishing. Don't be surprised if you catch a largemouth bass one cast and a redfish on the next, then a bream, then a sea trout. The tides are very influential.

Various creeks, channels, and rivers wind through the grassy marsh around the park. These waterways make for fun exploration in a canoe, a kayak, or even a paddleboard, all of which can be rented in the park for a very reasonable rate. Obtain a free fishing map of the area at the park office before you explore.

Being surrounded by a wildlife refuge has its advantages. Ochlockonee is a wildlife viewer's paradise. Birders come from all over. Deer, bobcats, and even a

bear or two have been known to call this park home. The Pine Flatwoods Trail makes a loop through the center of the park. Beware of a sometimes-wet section of the trail that crosses over a marsh. A connector trail makes this loop accessible from the picnic area or the campground. Another trail runs along the Ochlockonee River behind the campground and ends at the boat ramp. The watery vistas are awesome.

There is a swimming area that is roped off near the outstanding picnic area. Have a meal beneath the shady oaks while looking over the water and marshlands beyond. An L-shaped dock extends out into the middle of the river. I watched a memorable sunrise there.

Other features nearby are Wakulla Springs and St. Marks Wildlife Refuge. Wakulla Springs is one of the world's

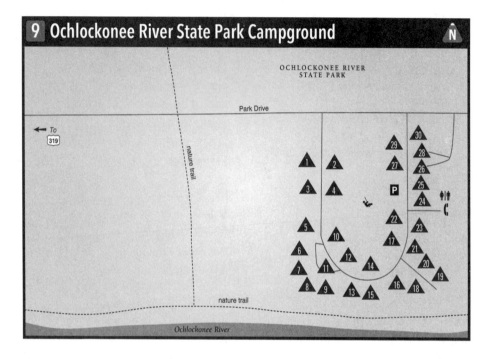

9 Ochlockonee River State Park Campground

OCHLOCKONEE RIVER
STATE PARK

Park Drive

← To 319

nature trail

nature trail

Ochlockonee River

largest natural springs. The water is incredibly clear. Take the glass-bottom boat tour and you can see the fossilized mastodon bones and the spring cavern 100 feet below! At St. Marks, stop by the visitor center and then head out to Pelican Point.

This is primarily a summertime campground. Weekends can fill, but

Ochlockonee always has a relaxed pace. Winter may see a few visitors from the North. Once people come here, they realize what a quiet place it is. If you like to be serenaded to sleep by frogs and crickets instead of cars and trains, Ochlockonee River Campground is the place to come.

:: Getting There

From Sopchoppy, drive south on US 319 for 4 miles. Ochlockonee River State Park will be on your left.

GPS COORDINATES   N30° 0′ 18.6″ W84° 28′ 44.2″

10

Pine Log State Forest Campground

Want to avoid the busy beach campgrounds and enjoy woodland camping? Then stay here.

Pine Log is an intimate 20-site lakeside campground, as well as a primitive camping area with three campsites along Pine Log Creek. The vicinity is quiet and relaxed. If you want to avoid the busy beach campgrounds and you enjoy woodland camping, stay here. The budget minded can stay at one of the primitive sites and go to the public beaches of Panama City Beach.

You'll pass the reassuring site of the ranger's residence on Longleaf Road as you enter the Pine Log Recreation Area. The sandy lane swings right around East Lake. The campground begins with a series of eight campsites overlooking the lake. Seven of the eight sites are directly lakeside. Overhead is a canopy of longleaf pine. The understory is sorely lacking between campsites. However, the sites have adequate spaciousness and a steady breeze rolling in off the lake.

The campground road veers away from the lake, but four more sites overlook the lake before the road turns completely away from the water. These campsites are especially roomy and aren't as coveted as the first lakeside sites. The ground cover here is more grass than sand.

The campground road turns to the left, and there are campsites on both sides of the road, resting in a more heavily wooded area. These sites will be warmer in winter. If you like privacy, camp here because this area is obviously less frequented.

The campground as a whole is never really busy. Weekdays are always quiet. Spring and summer weekends can see a fair number of campers. Because all the campsites have water and electricity, some snowbirds will stop over during the winter months. Summer is sporadic depending on the heat.

:: Ratings

BEAUTY: ★ ★ ★
PRIVACY: ★ ★
SPACIOUSNESS: ★ ★ ★
QUIET: ★ ★ ★ ★
SECURITY: ★ ★ ★ ★ ★
CLEANLINESS: ★ ★ ★ ★

:: Key Information

ADDRESS: Pine Log State Forest
5583-A Longleaf Road
Ebro, FL 32437

OPERATED BY: Florida Division
of Forestry

CONTACT: 850-535-2888, fresh
fromflorida.com/Divisions-Offices
/Florida-Forest-Service/Our-Forests
/State-Forests/Pine-Log-State-Forest

OPEN: Year-round

SITES: 20 developed, 3 primitive

EACH SITE: Tent pad, picnic table, fire
ring, water, electricity

ASSIGNMENT: First come, first served;
and by reservation

REGISTRATION: Self-registration
on-site

FACILITIES: Showers, flush toilets

PARKING: At campsites only

FEE: $15/night developed, $5/night
primitive

ELEVATION: 20'

RESTRICTIONS:

■ **Pets:** On maximum 6-foot leash only

■ **Fires:** In fire rings only

■ **Alcohol:** Prohibited

■ **Vehicles:** None

■ **Other:** 14-day stay limit in a 30-day
period

Back the other way on Longleaf Road are the primitive campsites. They are widely separated along a 1-mile stretch of bumpy sand road passable by an ordinary passenger car. A sign nailed to a tree designates each site. Beyond the small parking spot is a short path that leads to the campsites. Each site features only a tent spot and a fire ring. The coffee-colored and sand-bottomed Pine Log Creek meanders by on the way to the Gulf. Each of these sites offers solitude not only from the main campground but from each of the other primitive sites as well. Be apprised that you are not entitled to use the restroom or shower facilities in the main campground.

This makes a great place to stop if you are on the way to the Gulf, and also a great inland site from which to make salty side trips. Plus, Pine Log has recreational opportunities of its own. East Lake has a swimming area. Both East and West Lakes offer good freshwater fishing. Only hand-launched boats without power motors are allowed on the lakes—canoes and the like. You can also canoe Pine Log Creek. Put in near the primitive sites and take out at a boat ramp a few miles down, as shown on the map at the campground.

Three trails start at the campground itself. The Campground Trail makes a 2-mile loop around both lakes and the campground. The 4-mile Edgar "Dutch" Tiemann Nature Trail loops all the way down along Pine Log Creek and back. Then there's the 9-mile Crooked Creek Trail, which starts a mile south of the campground on the east side of FL 79. Both "Dutch" and Crooked Creek are multiuse,

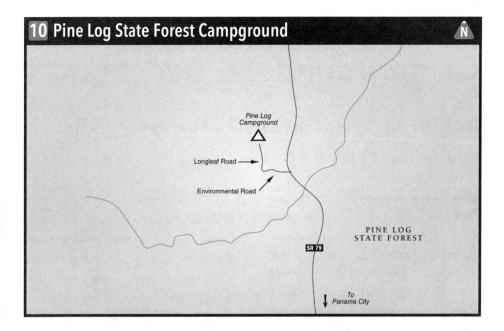

10 Pine Log State Forest Campground

Pine Log Campground

Longleaf Road →

Environmental Road

SR 79

PINE LOG
STATE FOREST

To Panama City

meaning both hikers and mountain bikers are welcome. An 8-mile section of the Florida National Scenic Trail runs through this section of the forest.

On my trip, I stayed at primitive campsite 1. The pine forest descended toward the creek and became dominated by cypress trees near the camp. The day was overcast and cool as I started an early morning hike on the Tiemann Trail. I liked just walking right from my campsite to the trail. The afternoon cleared, so I made the half-hour drive down to the beach, returning to Pine Log in time to cook a campfire shish kebab before turning in for the night.

The quiet atmosphere of Pine Log lured me into an extra night's stay. I enjoyed the primitive campsite and the chance to enjoy both the saltwater and freshwater ecosystems. I recommend that you do the same.

:: Getting There

From Panama City, drive west on US 98 for 10 miles to FL 79. Turn right on FL 79 and follow it 12.6 miles to Environmental Road. Turn left on Environmental Road and follow it 0.3 mile to Longleaf Road. Turn right on Longleaf Road and then into the campground in a short distance.

GPS COORDINATES   N30° 25′ 20.7″ W85° 52′ 15.2″

11

Rocky Bayou State Park Campground

Rocky Bayou Campground has the advantages of salt water without all the saltwater crowds.

Overlooking an arm of Choctaw hatchee Bay, Rocky Bayou has a nice waterfront campground that features both land- and water-oriented recreational opportunities. It is one of Florida's smaller state parks, so don't plan on an extended stay unless you just want to curl up with a good book at a quiet campground. Rocky Bayou is perfect for that.

The 42 campsites are situated on a large, paved loop road that passes through a sand pine forest. Both sand pine and longleaf pine mix in with live oaks to make a shady campground. A thick understory of yaupon holly, wax myrtle, and saw palmetto combine to provide fine campsite privacy. A few southern magnolias add to the flora.

:: Ratings

BEAUTY: ★ ★ ★ ★
PRIVACY: ★ ★ ★
SPACIOUSNESS: ★ ★ ★ ★
QUIET: ★ ★
SECURITY: ★ ★ ★ ★
CLEANLINESS: ★ ★ ★ ★

The camping area is mostly flat, with a very slight slope angling toward Rocky Bayou. The first 11 campsites on the outside of the loop are the largest and are where tent campers will want to be. The 14 sites across the road are more compact. These are the less-desirable sites in which to stay.

As the loop turns, you'll pass the short pathway to the nature trails and Puddin' Head Lake. The next 11 campsites are on the inside of the loop. They are close together but are where the RVs like to congregate. These campsites have the advantage of overlooking Rocky Bayou across a grassy lawn. There is also a picnic pavilion for campers near a swimming beach. The road passes the heated and air-conditioned comfort station on the inside of the loop, then comes to six more campsites on the inside of the loop.

Rocky Bayou Campground is quiet most of the year. During the winter, travelers will use it as a stopover spot. The campground starts to get busy in mid-March and stays full on warm weekends until September. Weekdays during this

:: Key Information

ADDRESS: Rocky Bayou State Park
4281 FL 20
Niceville, FL 32578

OPERATED BY: Florida State Parks

CONTACT: 850-833-9144, floridastate
parks.org; reservations 800-326-3521,
reserveamerica.com

OPEN: Year-round

SITES: 42

EACH SITE: Picnic table, fire ring,
water, electricity

ASSIGNMENT: First come, first served;
or reserve online

REGISTRATION: At ranger station

FACILITIES: Hot showers, flush toilets

PARKING: At campsites only

FEE: $16/night

ELEVATION: Sea level

RESTRICTIONS:

■ **Pets:** On 6-foot leash
■ **Fires:** In fire rings only
■ **Alcohol:** Prohibited
■ **Vehicles:** None
■ **Other:** 14-day stay limit

time are about half full. So unless you arrive at the campground at 5 p.m. on a warm Saturday, you are likely to find a good campsite. Once you find a good campsite, reserve it the next trip.

Rocky Bayou has more than a mile of shoreline to enjoy. There are two primary swimming areas: down from the campground pavilion at the campground and near the picnic area. Swim with someone for safety, as there is no lifeguard on duty. Anglers have their own launch to access the saltwater species swimming about Rocky Bayou. These waters are part of the Rocky Bayou Aquatic Preserve and are becoming a popular canoeing and kayaking destination.

I personally liked Puddin' Head Lake. With a name like that, what's there not to love? It was created by beavers—you can see the dam just steps away from

the campground. The water is clear and full of freshwater fish. If you bring a canoe, you'll probably bring out fish.

Another way to check out Puddin' Head Lake is the Sand Pine Trail. Make sure to stop by the ranger station to get the well-written handout for the Rocky Bayou nature trails. Sand Pine Trail skirts the eastern edge of the lake. Look for fish in the water, and don't miss the second beaver dam on the upper stretches of the lake.

The Rocky Bayou Trail starts at Puddin' Head Lake and makes its own loop. Part of the trail winds along the waters of Rocky Bayou. The Red Cedar Trail begins near the picnic area and traverses an area of southern magnolia, sand pine, live oak, and, of course, red cedar.

If you want to get right on the beach, take the Mid-Bay Bridge, FL 293, over

11 Rocky Bayou State Park Campground

N

Rocky Bayou

To
Niceville

SR 20

ROCKY BAYOU
STATE PARK

*Rocky Bayou
Campground*

path to
Puddin'
Head
Lake

11 nonelectric sites
31 electric sites

to Henderson Beach State Recreation Area in Destin. It has the famed sugar-white sand beaches for which this area is known. Picnic shelters and bathhouses are provided for your comfort.

Rocky Bayou has the advantages of salt water without all the crowds. You can enjoy the Gulf and return here. And at Rocky Bayou, there is ample recreation without ever leaving your campsite.

:: Getting There

From Niceville, take FL 20 East for 5 miles. Rocky Bayou State Park will be on your left.

GPS COORDINATES   N30° 29' 49.1" W86° 25' 39.6"

12

St. Andrews State Park Campground

St. Andrews State Park has superior natural features but a large, average campground.

The **blue-and-green** waters here contrast brilliantly with the white beach. Shell Island, one of the few pristine barrier islands left, is one of the best examples of the real, natural Florida in the state. The campground has its share of good sites, but it is so big it sometimes seems like a city of its own.

There are two campgrounds that are really so close that they are more like one. In general, the camping area is beneath a pine forest between Grand Lagoon and some old sand dunes. Saw palmetto forms a light understory. The campground is open, and you can see from one site to the next. A recent road repaving caused many trees to be cut down, but there is adequate shade overhead.

:: Ratings

BEAUTY: ★ ★ ★ ★
PRIVACY: ★ ★ ★
SPACIOUSNESS: ★ ★ ★
QUIET: ★ ★
SECURITY: ★ ★ ★ ★ ★
CLEANLINESS: ★ ★ ★ ★

The first area is called Lagoon Campground. It has 100 campsites. Thirty-one sites are waterfront. Some are directly on the water, while others have a section of saw grass between the water and the campsite. The campsites away from the water abut some attractive sand dunes that provide shade but cut down on the ocean breeze, which can be good or bad, according to the season.

There is one loop in the Grand Lagoon. The 22 campsites on the inside of the loop are well forested, but they have neither a dune by them nor a waterfront view. Two fully equipped comfort stations serve the lagoon campground. Overall, the campsites in the Lagoon Campground are smaller and closer together than the sites in the Pine Grove Campground.

Pine Grove Campground has 75 campsites, 22 of which are waterfront. This area has recently been burned over; the undergrowth is coming back and eventually will be thicker. There are three separate loops in Pine Grove. Each loop has its own fully equipped comfort station; the farthest loop has laundry facilities as well.

:: Key Information

ADDRESS: St. Andrews State Park 4607 State Park Lane Panama City, FL 32408	**FACILITIES:** Hot showers, flush toilets, camp store, laundry
OPERATED BY: Florida State Parks	**PARKING:** At campsites only
CONTACT: 850-233-5140, floridastate parks.org; reservations 800-326-3521, reserveamerica.com	**FEE:** $28/night
	ELEVATION: Sea level
OPEN: Year-round	**RESTRICTIONS:**
SITES: 175	■ **Pets:** Prohibited
EACH SITE: Picnic table, fire ring, water, electricity	■ **Fires:** In fire rings only
ASSIGNMENT: Assigned by ranger	■ **Alcohol:** Prohibited
REGISTRATION: Online or at park entrance booth	■ **Vehicles:** None
	■ **Other:** 14-day stay limit

The 30 campsites on the inside of the loops have the least privacy. The farthest loop has an odd configuration of campsites that allows the most privacy, especially in such a large campground that is going to have a significant amount of casual drive-by traffic.

St. Andrews is busy from March, when the college spring-breakers come, and through the summer, when vacationing families take over. Starting in September, the campground slows back down. Winter has its share of snowbirds. This is when the number of RVs will be at its peak. Unfortunately, tents and RVs aren't separated.

When you come to St. Andrews, ask to drive through the campground to select your site. There are campsites that range from superb to some real dogs. That is the only problem when you reserve a site online—you can't pick your site. However, once you arrive, you can try to change to a better campsite. Be aware of the fact that the campground is not an all-natural experience. It looks out over the civilized mainland.

Once here, you'll see why so many other campers have joined you. Take the mandatory walk on the beach. Huge dunes rise around the jetty area. From atop the dunes you can see the water range in color from green to blue as the water depth changes. These dunes descend to water level.

Across the jetty is Shell Island. In the warmer months, a ferry runs to the island every 30 minutes. This place is the getaway from the getaway. It is 7 miles around the island. The farther you ferry from St. Andrews, the more isolated Shell Island gets. This is what Florida used to look like before time-share condos and T-shirt shops took over. Simply put, it's spectacular.

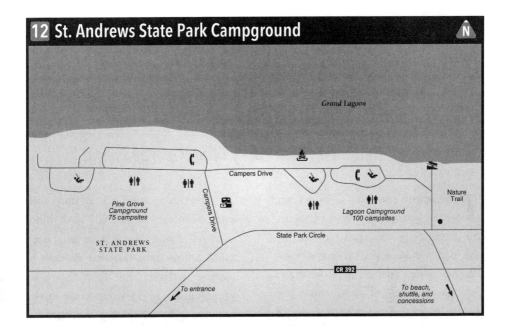

12 St. Andrews State Park Campground

The main beach is where swimmers and sunbathers congregate. Behind the jetty is a swimming area without all the wave action. Anglers can be seen on the jetty, the Gulf fishing pier, and the Grand Lagoon fishing pier.

If you get tired of walking the beach, try the Gator Lake Nature Trail or the Pine Flatwoods Nature Trail. Both are short walks through oceanside ecosystems. Be sure to check out the old turpentine still. It is located near the boat ramp that extends into Grand Lagoon. Canoes are also for rent here. If you forget supplies, there is a park store that sells goodies and ice.

The campground at St. Andrews is big, but the natural beauty is big too. Just pick a good campsite, and remember that the campground isn't as populated as most of the places where we live.

:: Getting There

From Panama City, drive west on US 98, cross the bridge over West Bay, and continue a short distance to County Road 3031. Turn left on CR 3031 and follow it 4 miles to CR 392. Turn left on CR 392 and shortly turn into St. Andrews State Park.

GPS COORDINATES   N30° 7' 51.7" W85° 44' 14.4"

13

St. George Island State Park Campground

Beach lovers can really appreciate this park. If only the campground matched the scenery of St. George Island.

The eastern end of St. George Island is sand, sea, and sky. As you drive into the entrance, white sand blows across the road and waves roll up on the beach. Patches of sea oats cling to the dunes. Sunlight reflects off land and water. Beach lovers can really appreciate this park. If only the campground matched the scenery of St. George Island.

That is not to say the campground isn't worth pitching a tent. It is. It just doesn't match the raw beauty of St. George Island State Park. Turn left onto the campground road 4 miles beyond the park entrance. You'll pass a marsh and enter the long, narrow campground loop. It has 60 campsites; all but 11 are on the outside of the loop.

:: Ratings

BEAUTY: ★ ★ ★
PRIVACY: ★ ★ ★
SPACIOUSNESS: ★ ★ ★
QUIET: ★ ★ ★ ★
SECURITY: ★ ★ ★ ★ ★
CLEANLINESS: ★ ★ ★ ★

The campground has an open feel, even though there are tall slash pines scattered about. The first 28 sites back up to a pine flatwoods that changes to marshy wetland. The holly known as yaupon grows in clumps to break up the campground. Tall grass grows right up to some campsites that abut the marsh. These sites have a buggy look to them.

As the loop curves around, the campsites are nearer to the dunes. Small pine trees and hodgepodge clumps of brush divide the sites, yet the area still conveys a feeling of openness. Campsite privacy is compromised somewhat. Adequate space is provided for all campsites at St. George. The campsites in the center of the loop are even more open. They are next to the two fully equipped bathhouses. Crushed oyster shells and grass form the ground cover for the campground.

Despite not being separate designed areas for RVs and tents, you probably won't see too many RVs except during the winter months when snowbirds use St. George Island as a stopover spot while heading for points farther south.

:: Key Information

ADDRESS: St. George Island State Park, 1900 East Gulf Beach Dr. St. George Island, FL 32328

OPERATED BY: Florida State Parks

CONTACT: 850-927-2111, floridastate parks.org; reservations 800-326-3521, reserveamerica.com

OPEN: Year-round

SITES: 60

EACH SITE: Picnic table, fire ring, water, electricity

ASSIGNMENT: First come, first served; and by reservation

REGISTRATION: Online or at park entrance booth

FACILITIES: Showers, flush toilets, dump station

PARKING: At campsites and extra car parking

FEE: $24/night

ELEVATION: Sea level

RESTRICTIONS:

■ **Pets:** On 6-foot leash maximum

■ **Fires:** In fire rings only

■ **Alcohol:** In designated areas only

■ **Vehicles:** None

■ **Other:** 14-day stay limit

Remember to store your food properly here. Bold raccoons will come out during the day and rob you of your precious goodies. During my visit, I saw three raccoons raid a campsite while the tenants were away.

After you've stored your food, the first place you should head is for the beach. It is very wide and 9 miles long. Beachcombers can walk until their legs fail them. Dunes rise and fall on the narrow spit of land. If you really want to get wild, walk to East Point. This is the most pristine part of the island; however, be prepared for a sandy trek that will be surprisingly challenging. There is a four-wheel-drive road that can take you to East Point—get a permit at the ranger station. The views over Apalachicola Sound, the Gulf, and nearby Dog Island are worth

the walk. Anglers can catch flounder, redfish, whiting, and sea trout.

Shade-seeking woodland hikers can take the 2.5-mile trail out to Gap Point. This trail passes through a live oak hammock and pine flatwoods. It starts at the back of the campground loop. Remember, this is a one-way hike, so be ready to hike 2.5 miles back.

You may see some birds here. There are native feathered friends, such as terns and plovers, and many migratory visitors making St. George a stopover spot. The campground sounded like a winged sing-along when I was there.

If you leave the island, go to Apalachicola for some very fresh seafood. The water that's all around you, Apalachicola Bay, is some of the world's most productive waters for oysters and other edible

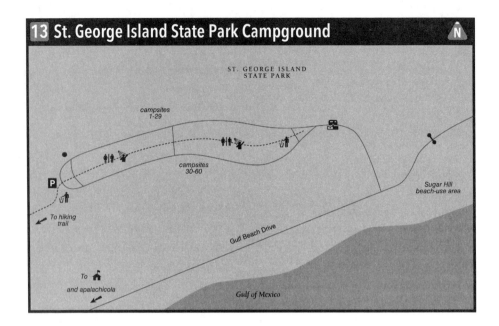

sea critters. You can't get seafood much fresher than you will get it in Apalachicola. Plus, you will get to take in some of the native culture. It's a Southern country town by the sea. While you are in town, visit the John Gorrie Museum. He invented the ice machine. It's all part of the St. George Island experience.

:: Getting There

From Apalachicola, drive east on US 98 and cross John Gorrie Memorial Bridge. Turn right on County Road 300 and cross St. George Sound to St. George Island. Then turn left on Gulf Beach Drive and follow it 4 miles to the entrance of St. George Island State Park.

GPS COORDINATES   N29° 41' 24" W84° 47' 4"

14

St. Joseph Peninsula State Park Campground

The huge sand dunes and miles of beach and woods will beckon you.

St. Joseph Peninsula State Park is a narrow spit of land that juts out into the Gulf of Mexico. It is surrounded by water. A wilderness preserve covers the last 1,650 acres of the sliver of land. The huge sand dunes and miles of beach and woods will beckon you. One of the two park campgrounds is ideal for tent campers.

As you drive on the narrow expanse of land, you can see water on both sides. You wonder, where are they going to put a campground? Soon you come to Gulf Breeze Camp. It has 59 campsites in an open area between a marsh and sand dunes. Pine trees grow about the area, but it is not a forest by any means. The center of the loop is grassy with a

:: Ratings

BEAUTY: ★ ★ ★ ★ ★
PRIVACY: ★ ★ ★ ★
SPACIOUSNESS: ★ ★
QUIET: ★ ★ ★
SECURITY: ★ ★ ★ ★ ★
CLEANLINESS: ★ ★ ★ ★

smattering of palms. The outer part of the loop is sandy, with a light understory. The campsites are wide enough to pull an RV in. Two crossroads bisect the loop so RVs can pull in and out.

There are two bathhouses for this loop. The only advantage this area has over the other camping area is its proximity to the beach, but the difference is negligible compared with the negatives of this loop. Stay here only if there are no other sites in the other loop.

Shady Pines Camp is farther into the park. The campsite ratings are for this loop only. It has 60 campsites in a thick forest of longleaf pine, sand live oak, and sabal palm, stretched out on an oval loop. Attractive, sizable campsites are on either side of the loop. A dense understory of palmetto, yaupon, and other brush rises high and shields the campsites from one another. Where there's no brush, there is grass.

Nearly all of the campsites on the second half of Shady Pines Camp are on the inside of the loop. They can be quite hemmed in by the brush, yet that is a positive trait. Four larger campsites are

:: Key Information

ADDRESS: St. Joseph Peninsula State
Park, 8899 Cape San Blas Road
Port St. Joe, FL 32456

OPERATED BY: Florida State Parks

CONTACT: 850-227-1327, floridastate
parks.org; reservations 800-326-3521,
reserveamerica.com

OPEN: Year-round

SITES: 119

EACH SITE: Picnic table, fire ring,
water spigot, electricity

ASSIGNMENT: Online or assigned by
ranger

REGISTRATION: Online or at park
entrance booth

FACILITIES: Showers, flush toilets

PARKING: At campsite only

FEE: $24/night

ELEVATION: Sea level

RESTRICTIONS:

■ Pets: Prohibited

■ Fires: In fire rings only

■ Alcohol: Prohibited

■ Vehicles: None

on the outside of the loop in a low spot that could prove uncomfortable during a rainstorm. The only negative aspect of these sites is a subdued ocean breeze. Nearly all the sites here from 104 to 117 are designated tent only. All the others are designated tent or RV. Two comfort stations serve this entire loop. Warning: Do not leave any food out here—the raccoons are persistent and sneaky.

It is just a short walk from either campground to the beach. Here you will find miles of white sand, bordered by some of the highest dunes in Florida. Walk until you find your own relaxation spot. Surf-fishing can be done in the Gulf or in St. Joseph Bay. Sea trout fishing in the bay can be excellent. If you like to hunt for shells, go to the bay side. I have never seen so many sand dollars in one place in all my life. Only the dead white shells may be collected.

There is a boat launch at the marina, where canoes can be rented as well. A ranger has to approve the rental of a canoe, which is dependent on water conditions. Two nature trails serve the park. The Bay Trail leaves the picnic area and explores the woods and marsh of the bay side of the peninsula. The Coastal Hammock Trail starts at the park entrance and winds through an oceanside woodland that is rapidly disappearing in areas surrounding it.

But the primary exploratory attraction is the St. Joseph Wilderness Preserve. It covers the northern 7 miles of the peninsula and has the biggest sand dunes of them all. A freshwater marsh waters wildlife such as deer, raccoon, gray fox, and bobcat. Birders will be rewarded with sightings too. Permits are required for overnight camping in the wilderness. They are available at the entrance station.

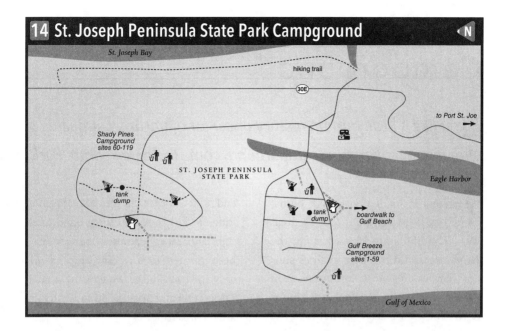

14 St. Joseph Peninsula State Park Campground

There are three ways to explore the preserve. You can walk the Gulf beach, the more difficult bay beach, or the center of the island via an old fire road. I've done them all and like to hike the fire road best. This is because it intersects the other roads and you can reach the Gulf or the bay depending on your whim. You can even devise a loop of your own. The fire road starts at the end of Cabin Road.

Every season offers something special here. Get reservations in spring and summer. Fall can be a special time, with warm days and cool nights. Winter offers solitude. No matter when you visit, you should have a wonderful experience. Accessible natural vistas are uncommon in Florida.

:: Getting There

From Port St. Joe, go east on US 98. After 3 miles, turn right on FL 30 and follow it 8 miles. Take the sharp right turn on FL 30E and follow it 9 miles into the park.

GPS COORDINATES   N29° 46′ 30″ W85° 24′ 25″

15

Torreya State Park Campground

If you like a little human history and a lot of nature, complete with a quiet, attractive campground, come to Torreya State Park.

Torreya is loaded with high bluffs; even the campground sports a great view. The bluffs are located along the Apalachicola River. Their inclines support hardwoods more commonly seen in the Southern Appalachian Mountains. The park is also the home of the rare Torreya tree that grows only in this area. If that isn't enough, this surprising state park is home of the antebellum Gregory House, where tours will open your eyes to Panhandle plantation life.

The Weeping Ridge Camping Area is a peaceful island surrounded on three sides by steep bluffs. Thirty campsites spur off the outside of the teardrop-shaped, sand loop road. The tall forest overhead is a mixture of pine, live oak, and a few other hardwoods. Weeping Ridge is fairly open on the ground level. But landscaped campsite buffers have been planted to increase campsite privacy and continue growing by the season. These trees and bushes add to an already attractive setting.

The first 16 campsites are fairly close to one another but extend far back from the road, creating long and narrow campsites. Each site backs up to a bluff. Just beyond the 16th campsite, the sand road curves and opens up to a rare Florida vista. A grassy yard with two benches lies beneath some really large hardwoods. To your north is an expanse of land and distance that beckons you to scan the horizon.

Past the vista are much wider sites, yet every bit as deep as the previous ones. These sites back up to a bluff as well. A clean comfort station interrupts the sequence of campsites on the outside of the loop.

The final six campsites are the largest in the campground. They have sizable grassy areas beneath the trees. If you have a large family or a lot of gear, then these sites are for you. There is also a special

:: Ratings

BEAUTY: ★ ★ ★ ★
PRIVACY: ★ ★ ★
SPACIOUSNESS: ★ ★ ★
QUIET: ★ ★ ★ ★ ★
SECURITY: ★ ★ ★ ★ ★
CLEANLINESS: ★ ★ ★ ★

:: Key Information

ADDRESS: Torreya State Park
HC 2, Box 70, 2576 NW
Torreya Park Road, Bristol, FL 32321

OPERATED BY: Florida State Parks

CONTACT: 850-643-2674, floridastate
parks.org; reservations 800-326-3521,
reserveamerica.com

OPEN: Year-round

SITES: 30

EACH SITE: Picnic table, fire ring,
water, electricity

ASSIGNMENT: Online or first come,
first served

REGISTRATION: At campground
meetinghouse

FACILITIES: Hot showers, flush toilets

PARKING: At campsites only

FEE: $16/night

ELEVATION: 250'

RESTRICTIONS:

■ **Pets:** Prohibited

■ **Fires:** In fire rings only

■ **Alcohol:** Prohibited

■ **Vehicles:** None

treat for those who camp here—one of the rare Torreya trees lies along the road between campsites 28 and 29. The small evergreen looks out of place in the surrounding forest.

The center of the campground has a grassy lawn beneath the pines. It houses the Meeting House, which hosts infrequent camp functions and doubles as the registration location. Torreya State Park is rarely busy. It lies at the end of a road in a rural area. This makes for a quiet, peaceful camping experience.

The first thing to do once you set up camp is to visit the Gregory House. This house was actually across the Apalachicola River at one time. It was moved to its present location in the 1930s. The plantation of Jason Gregory was built in 1849 and thrived on slave labor until the Civil War. It is furnished with items from the 1850s. It's worth your time to take the ranger-led

tour, offered at 10 a.m. weekdays and three times on weekends. The view from the front of the house looks down on the river and the former location of the house.

From the front of the house you can take the Apalachicola River Bluffs Trail, designated a National Recreation Trail. It drops down off the steep bluff and passes old Confederate gun pits that once protected the river route, important in those times. The trail leads right down along the river itself.

The park has two long-distance trails, thanks to a recent land acquisition. There are two loops, approximately 7 miles each. They both pass through the many plant communities represented in the park and have more hills than just about any other hiking trail in the state.

A shorter trail starts right at the campground. The Weeping Ridge Trail leads down a bluff to a small waterfall. I

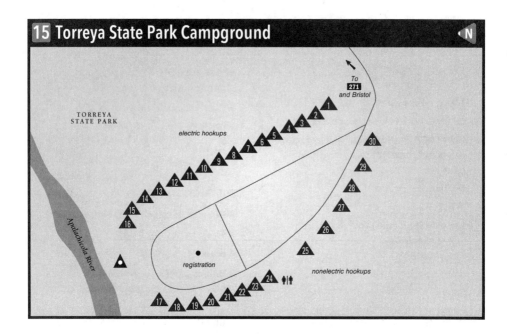

15 Torreya State Park Campground

walked this little gem early in the morning, after a significant rain. The little falls was dropping for all it was worth.

I came back to the nearly abandoned campground wondering why more people don't come here. I visit this park on a regular basis. The Apalachicola River below has emerged as a paddling destination the past few years. I have floated the entire Apalachicola from its origin near the Georgia state line to the Gulf.

A canoe or kayak trip down this big river would enhance your Torreya experience. The hilly terrain is pleasantly unique for the state. The rare Torreya tree, along with another rare evergreen—the Florida yew—make this place special. As a matter of fact, the world-record Florida yew is in this park. If you like a little human history and a lot of nature, complete with a quiet, attractive campground, come to Torreya State Park.

:: Getting There

From Bristol, take FL 12 north 7 miles. Turn left on County Road 1641 and follow it 7 miles to Torreya State Park.

GPS COORDINATES   N30° 34' 8.9"   W84° 57' 0.4"

16

Wright Lake Recreation Area Campground

This campground offers the best of two worlds. It is in a remote section of a scenic national forest but has the amenities of a more developed campground.

Wright **Lake Campground** has been completely revamped by the US Forest Service. Far from the civilized world, Wright Lake is a well-kept secret among locals and those who stumble onto it. This campground offers the best of two worlds. It is in a remote section of a scenic national forest but has the amenities of a more developed campground. There are outdoor activities within walking and driving distance.

Once you find Wright Lake Campground, you will see why national forest aficionados come back time and again. It is on a side road off a dead-end road. The campground is in a teardrop-shaped loop beneath a stately forest of mature pines.

:: Ratings

BEAUTY: ★ ★ ★ ★
PRIVACY: ★ ★ ★
SPACIOUSNESS: ★ ★ ★ ★ ★
QUIET: ★ ★ ★ ★ ★
SECURITY: ★ ★ ★
CLEANLINESS: ★ ★ ★ ★

A parklike openness below the pines is broken up by patches of underbrush and small laurel oaks. Grass and pine needles carpet the camping area.

There are only 20 campsites, but there is enough room for 40. Space is no problem here. The daunting size of the campground means more site privacy. The seven campsites on the inside of the loop are more open. Thick brush separates most of the campsites on the outside of the loop. There has even been some tastefully decorative landscaping of Wright Lake since its makeover.

Everything at each campsite is kept in good condition—fire ring, grill, picnic table, water spigot, and lantern post. All the sites are appealing, but water lovers may want to get the last four sites on the outside of the loop. They back up to Wright Lake.

A comfort station centers the loop. It has warm-water showers and flush toilets. Most of the old-timers at the campground have seen it evolve over many years from a free but rough camping area

:: Key Information

ADDRESS: Wright Lake Recreation Area, FL 20, P.O. Box 579 Bristol, FL 32321	**REGISTRATION:** Self-registration on-site
OPERATED BY: US Forest Service	**FACILITIES:** Hot showers, flush toilets
CONTACT: 850-643-2282, www.fs.usda.gov/apalachicola	**PARKING:** At campsites only
	FEE: $10/night
	ELEVATION: 20′
OPEN: Year-round	**RESTRICTIONS:**
SITES: 20	■ **Pets:** On 6-foot leash maximum
EACH SITE: Tent pad, picnic table, fire ring, grill, water spigot, lantern post	■ **Fires:** In fire rings only
	■ **Alcohol:** Prohibited
ASSIGNMENT: First come, first served; no reservations	■ **Vehicles:** None
	■ **Other:** 14-day stay limit

to the Apalachicola National Forest's best campground. A campground host is on-site most of the year and keeps things shipshape and safe.

I have seen it change myself and have been pleasantly surprised. I am of the opinion that you can't improve on the works of nature. Yet Wright Lake Campground proves to me that you can tastefully integrate the works of man into the works of nature.

With such a fine campground, the Forest Service had to come up with recreation to match. They have constructed the Wright Lake Trail, a 4.5-mile loop that covers the most interesting terrain in the area. The trail starts in the picnic area by the lake. The board at the beginning of the trail thoroughly explains each ecosystem, from cypress swamp to pine woods. It also shows where to look for wildlife as you walk this trail. The trail makes a

beeline for Owl Creek, then skirts several ponds, crosses pine flatwoods, and reemerges at Wright Lake. The Wright Lake Loop Trail travels a quarter mile and intersects the campground. Watch for red-cockaded woodpeckers, but you'll probably hear them before you see them.

Wright Lake is small but scenic. It doesn't even have a boat launch. This natural lake is made for kayaks and canoes. Since there is very little direct land access for the lake, paddlers have the advantage when it comes to casting their lines for bream, bass, and catfish.

Nearby Owl Creek offers swamp canoeing at its best. Put in at Hickory Landing, just down the road, and paddle upstream or downstream, then return— the current isn't too swift. Kennedy Creek, accessible from Cotton Landing, is also a great place for remote canoeing. Both creeks flow into the Apalachicola

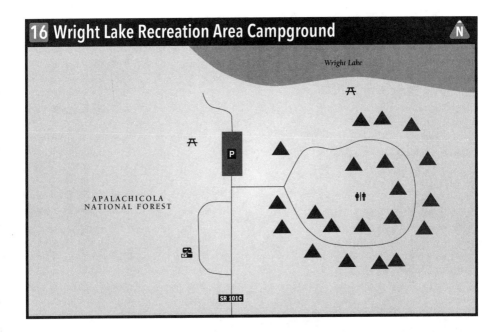

16 Wright Lake Recreation Area Campground

Wright Lake

APALACHICOLA
NATIONAL FOREST

SR 101C

River and have angling opportunities of their own.

Make sure to bring all of the supplies you will need. The hamlet of Sumatra has one small store, and it's a good 1-hour drive to a town of any size. If you must drive, take the Apalachee Savannahs Scenic Byway. It is FL 12 through the national forest. The open, wet meadows are botanically rich. South of Wright Lake on the byway is Fort Gadsden Historic Site. Here you'll find a museum that tells of the strategic importance of the Apalachicola River.

Wright Lake is a place to come to again and again. Just try to keep it a secret—once you find it.

:: Getting There

From Sumatra, take FL 65 south 2 miles. Turn right on FL 101 and drive about 2 miles. Turn right on FL 101-C and follow it about 0.3 mile. Wright Lake will be on your right.

GPS COORDINATES   N29° 59′ 58.7″ W85° 0′ 29.0″

Northern Florida

17

Anastasia State Park Campground

The windswept coastal forest, the lure of the beach, and the sense of history all combine to make Anastasia a worthwhile stop for anyone coming to the Sunshine State.

St. Augustine is noted for being the oldest city in the United States. Anastasia State Park should be noted for its campground set in a coastal hammock, its unspoiled beaches, and general marine character.

The 139 campsites suggest a large campground, but Anastasia is divided into seven distinct loops, all enveloped in the thickness of the coastal woods. These woods make each loop feels like its own distinct campground. The unusual forest is a product of its proximity to the ocean. Live oak is the primary tree here, but it's crowded by the smaller laurel oak. Palms fight for space and light, along with red cedar and southern magnolia. The bushy

:: Ratings

BEAUTY: ★ ★ ★ ★
PRIVACY: ★ ★ ★ ★
SPACIOUSNESS: ★ ★ ★
QUIET: ★ ★ ★
SECURITY: ★ ★ ★ ★ ★
CLEANLINESS: ★ ★ ★ ★

understory is primarily a plant called yaupon; it is a type of holly that makes an ideal campsite buffer. All this flora makes for a distinctly Florida forest.

As you pass the tiny camp store, you'll see the first loop, Coquina, on your left. Don't even bother—it's RV headquarters. Turn right to access the other six loops. All of the loops on the main campground road run east–west in a long and narrow pattern. Two loops each share a bathhouse, located between them. The bathhouses all have hot showers and flush toilets.

After Coquina, the next two loops are Sea Bean and Queen Conch. Electricity has been added to these former tent-only loops, but they are still the best choices for tent campers because they offer the best in campsite privacy in a dense maritime forest. However, the thick forest cuts down on site spaciousness, but the trade-off is more than worth it.

The next two loops, Shark Eye and Sand Dollar, have larger campsites and usually offer a mixed bag of tents, pop-ups, and a few RVs. The final two loops,

:: Key Information

ADDRESS: Anastasia State Park
300 Anastasia Park Rd.
St. Augustine, FL 32080

OPERATED BY: Florida State Parks

CONTACT: 904-461-2033,
floridastateparks.org;
reservations 800-326-3521,
reserveamerica.com

OPEN: Year-round

SITES: 139

EACH SITE: Picnic table, fire ring,
water spigot, electricity

ASSIGNMENT: Online or by ranger

REGISTRATION: By phone, online, at
park entrance, or at ranger station

FACILITIES: Hot showers, flush toilets,
camp store, Wi-Fi

PARKING: At campsites and extra car
parking

FEE: $28/night year-round

ELEVATION: Sea level

RESTRICTIONS:

■ **Pets:** On 6-foot leash

■ **Fires:** In fire rings only

■ **Alcohol:** Prohibited

■ **Vehicles:** None

Sea Urchin and Angel Wing, are much the same. These loops all share that beautiful, coastal hammock forest. For some reason, many campers like the few sites at the narrow curve of each loop the best. They are closest to the ocean but don't have an ocean view or direct ocean access. Maybe these campers can hear the waves better.

Early spring to late September is the more popular time to come. Some snowbirds set up camp here, despite it being in north Florida. Winter days can be very mild or cool. It's worth taking a chance, though, for solitude seekers. Summer-weekend campers are advised to get a campsite reservation in advance for peace of mind. Once securing a campsite, you can concentrate on what you are going to do when you get here.

The beach is the main focus at Anastasia. Although it is a short walk from the campground to the Atlantic, you can actually drive on the beach to your chosen spot if you want to. The beach is wide here and is backed by partially vegetated sand dunes. Swimmers, sunbathers, and beachcombers all find Anastasia to their liking. The northern end of the beach is for anglers, who surf-cast for pompano and whiting.

The tidal lagoon behind the beach is popular too. No swimming is allowed here in Salt Run, but canoes and windsurfing rigs are for rent. People fish for flounder, redfish, and sea trout in the calmer waters.

After you have received your fill of the beach, check in on the history here.

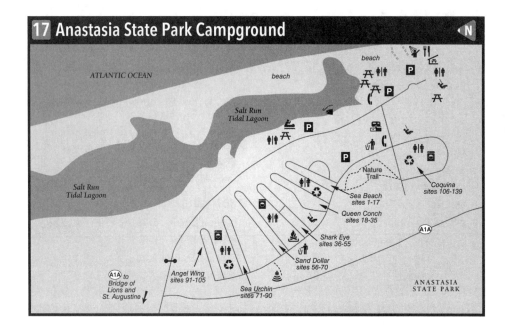

17 Anastasia State Park Campground

ATLANTIC OCEAN

beach

beach

Salt Run
Tidal Lagoon

Salt Run
Tidal Lagoon

Nature
Trail

Coquina
sites 106-139

Sea Beach
sites 1-17

Queen Conch
sites 18-35

Shark Eye
sites 36-55

Sand Dollar
sites 56-70

A1A to
Bridge of
Lions and
St. Augustine

Angel Wing
sites 91-105

Sea Urchin
sites 71-90

ANASTASIA
STATE PARK

A lesser-known but very interesting site is the Fort Matanzas National Monument. I enjoyed this side trip immensely. It is south of Anastasia on FL A1A. Matanzas is an old fort built in the 1700s by the British. A free boat tour takes you to the fort; a narrator gives an overview of this tower that once protected St. Augustine's back door.

Now you have to go to St. Augustine itself. There is another fort to see right in town, and trams will take you to see the primary sights. Then get out and walk around on your own. St. Augustine may be the oldest city in America, but it is certainly not the biggest. The city retains its small-town charm.

The windswept coastal forest, the lure of the beach, and the sense of history all combine to make Anastasia a worthwhile stop for anyone coming to the Sunshine State.

:: Getting There

From St. Augustine, drive south on FL A1A over the Bridge of Lions 2 miles. Anastasia State Recreation Area will be on your left.

GPS COORDINATES   N29° 51′ 54.8″ W81° 16′ 10.0″

18

Fort Clinch State Park Campground

Fort Clinch State Park centers around American military history amid a scenic maritime ecosystem.

Located in the most northeasterly corner of Florida, Fort Clinch State Park centers around American military history amid a scenic maritime ecosystem. The park encompasses a peninsula that is surrounded by salt water on three sides. The two park campgrounds are located in distinctly different environments, giving tent campers a choice of where to stay depending on weather and personal whim.

The Atlantic Beach Campground is situated a few hundred feet from the Atlantic Ocean. A boardwalk connects campers to the sea. The first 21 campsites are spread along the outside of an open loop. A few palm trees form the only campground vegetation. This area is exposed to the elements—and this can be good or bad, depending on the season and weather. In the winter, you may enjoy the warmth of the sun, but the bite of the wind may be too much. That very same wind may be a blessing when the bugs are biting. Summer's heat can melt you out here. However, the addition of five tent-only sites makes this loop more desirable. They are exposed, however, so consider a sunshade of some sort in addition to your tent.

The loop center is occupied by a fully equipped comfort station that has hot showers, flush toilets, and laundry facilities. There is no privacy on this loop, and the openness of the large campsites attracts a share of RVs. But if this area doesn't suit you, Fort Clinch offers another camping option.

The Amelia River Campground is on the other side of the peninsula. It faces out toward the Amelia River, a saltwater estuary that drains the area behind Fort Clinch. A maritime hardwood hammock of live oak, laurel oak, and myrtle oak offers every degree of shade not available in the Beach Camp Area. American holly,

:: Ratings

BEAUTY: ★ ★ ★
PRIVACY: ★ ★ ★
SPACIOUSNESS: ★ ★ ★
QUIET: ★ ★ ★ ★
SECURITY: ★ ★ ★ ★ ★
CLEANLINESS: ★ ★ ★ ★

:: Key Information

ADDRESS: Fort Clinch State Park 2601 Atlantic Ave. Fernandina Beach, FL 32034	**REGISTRATION:** Online or at park entrance booth
OPERATED BY: Florida State Parks	**FACILITIES:** Hot showers, flush toilets, laundry, soda machine
CONTACT: 904-277-7274, floridastate parks.org; reservations 800-326-3521, reserveamerica.com	**PARKING:** At campsites only
	FEE: $26/night year-round
	ELEVATION: Sea level
OPEN: Year-round	**RESTRICTIONS:**
SITES: 63	■ **Pets:** On 6-foot leash
EACH SITE: Picnic table, fire ring, water, electricity	■ **Fires:** In fire rings only
	■ **Alcohol:** Prohibited
ASSIGNMENT: Online or first come, first served	■ **Vehicles:** None
	■ **Other:** 14-day stay limit

yaupon, palmetto, and red cedar form a varied understory.

Depending on the wind direction, the Amelia River Campground can get a few ocean breezes of its own. The 40 campsites are stretched along both sides of the loop road. A few of the sites at the far side of the loop avail an obscured view of the Intracoastal Waterway. A small beach area looks out over the river.

A fully equipped comfort station with the same amenities as at the Beach Area Camp is located toward the river side of the loop. The Amelia River Campground attracts more tenters and is the preferred camping area. From my point of view, why not camp in the forest and access the beach at your whim?

And Fort Clinch has a great beach. The southern section has high dunes

between you and the rest of the mainland. Nearly a mile long, there is ample room for shellers, sunbathers, and surf-anglers. The extreme northeastern corner of the beach has a pier that extends into the Atlantic. You can also fish the marshy backside of the island.

The Willow Pond Nature Trail courses through the hardwood hammock in the center of the park—the forested in-between zone as the peninsula makes the transition from beach to marsh.

The highlight of the park is the actual Fort Clinch. Pay a small fee to pass through the museum. Look around the museum, then prepare to enter the fort itself. Fort Clinch overlooks the Cumberland Sound. It was occupied by both Confederate and Union forces during the Civil War.

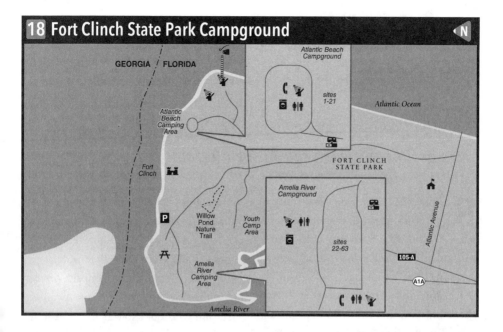

18 Fort Clinch State Park Campground

You can climb throughout the fort. Go into the bunkhouses. Look over the stockade. Go to one of the strategic points for fantastic views into the sound, the Atlantic, and the state of Georgia across the water. I felt like a kid running around, climbing staircases, going from one point to the next, checking out the cannons.

I was also lucky enough to witness one of the reenactments held at the fort. On the first full weekend of every month, park rangers dress as Union forces in the year 1864. Watch them go through the day-to-day chores of a soldier of the area. Families and children get in on the act too. It really adds to the authenticity of the fort. Candlelight tours of Fort Clinch are available, but you must make reservations. When you come to Fort Clinch, there will be no acting required to have a good time at this scenic and historic state park.

:: Getting There

From the town of Fernandina Beach, drive east on FL A1A (Atlantic Avenue) 1 mile. Just before you reach the beach, Fort Clinch State Park will be on your left.

GPS COORDINATES   N30° 41' 48.9" W81° 26' 23.5"

19

Gold Head Branch State Park Campground

The small campground is located on a hill and rests in flora native to this broken terrain.

Rolling hills in Florida? Yeah, that's right. Gold Head Branch State Park is located on what is known as the central ridge of Florida and boasts some serious elevation changes by Sunshine State standards. Steep ravines cut into these hills, adding more vertical variation. The small campground is located on a hill and rests in flora native to this broken terrain.

Gold Head Branch Campground is divided into three loops. The Sandhill Loop has 18 RV sites. Atop a hill, it is in an open area broken up by turkey oaks and longleaf pines. Turkey oaks get their name from the tip of the tree's leaf, which resembles a turkey foot. The ground cover consists of sand and wire grass.

:: Ratings

BEAUTY: ★ ★ ★
PRIVACY: ★ ★ ★
SPACIOUSNESS: ★ ★ ★ ★
QUIET: ★ ★ ★ ★ ★
SECURITY: ★ ★ ★ ★ ★
CLEANLINESS: ★ ★ ★ ★

Wire grass is native to this area and not nearly as bad as it sounds. The campsites encompass only three-quarters of the paved loop; seven sit on the inside.

There may be little campsite privacy, but the sites are very spacious. A comfort station with hot showers is in the loop's center. Some tent campers stay here, but it is mostly RVs in the Sandhill Loop.

The Turkey Oak Loop offers electricity and lacks RVs, which makes it by far the more appealing of the two loops. The packed-sand road is a bit bumpy as it passes through a shade-giving forest of longleaf pine, turkey oak, and sand live oak. The understory of wire grass, brush, and young tree seedlings is much thicker here, though the woods do thin out toward the end of the loop.

Campsites are very spacious, and many offer privacy that is more than adequate. Only four campsites are on the outside of the loop and back up to an open woodland. The comfort station is on the inside of the loop.

The bumpy dirt road and thick vegetation make Turkey Oak's 18 sites the tent

:: Key Information

ADDRESS: Gold Head Branch State Park, 6239 FL 21, Keystone Heights, FL 32656

OPERATED BY: Florida Park Service

CONTACT: 352-473-4701, floridastate parks.org; reservations 800-326-3521, reserveamerica.com

OPEN: Year-round

SITES: 65 electric, 9 nonelectric

EACH SITE: Picnic table, fire ring, water spigot

ASSIGNMENT: Online or by ranger

REGISTRATION: By phone or at park entrance booth

FACILITIES: Hot showers, flush toilets

PARKING: At campsites only

FEE: $20/night

ELEVATION: 125'

RESTRICTIONS:

■ **Pets:** On 6-foot leash maximum

■ **Fires:** In fire rings only

■ **Alcohol:** Prohibited

■ **Vehicles:** 2 vehicles/site

camper's choice. The Lakeview Camping Area offers an additional 36 sites; sites 38–56 and 71–74 are set up for RVs; sites 57–67 are nonelectric tent sites except for two electric wheelchair-accessible sites. Sites 68–70 have electrical hookups.

Why do they call it Gold Head? You'll have to come here to find out. Gold Head Branch is a series of clear springs at the bottom of a steep ravine. This ravine is an inverted island of moisture-loving plants. Water drains out of the sand hills, sinks into the ravine, then comes together to form Gold Head Branch, which flows into Little Lake Johnson.

Follow the boardwalk down to the ravine. Walk the Fern Trail and see the individual springs. You can also walk the Loblolly Trail and see the park's largest loblolly pines. Or walk the Ridge Trail,

a 1-mile hike that leads down to the old mill site. A man once dammed Gold Head Branch, using its energy to grind corn or to gin cotton.

A 3-mile portion of the Florida National Scenic Trail winds through the hills of the park. You'll see open stands of longleaf pine and turkey oak in the natural state of things on the central ridge. This open woodland, punctuated by the wire grass, is maintained by controlled burns. Outside the park, fire is generally suppressed, resulting in the loss of this natural habitat. Start at the entrance station and end near the park cabins.

Old fire roads and the old logging tram road are open to hikers and bikers. These paths crisscross the park. Get a map at the entrance booth so as not to get turned around.

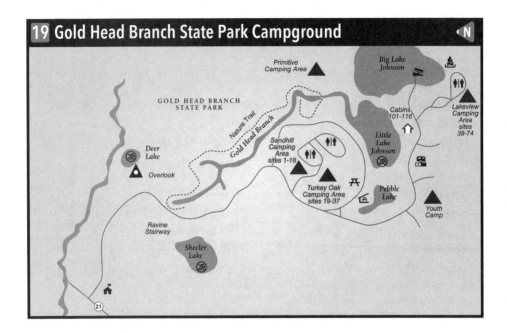

19 Gold Head Branch State Park Campground

All this hiking can make a body hot. There are five natural lakes in the park. Little Lake Johnson has a swimming beach. Canoes are for rent as well. Big Lake Johnson has a boat ramp and freshwater fishing. Sheeler Lake is open to fishing and swimming. The other two lakes are Deer Lake and Pebble Lake.

Summer weekends are the only time the campground regularly fills. Winter weekends can be intermittently busy. This is a different and special area, with a campground in an equally unusual setting. The Florida hills are calling you. Can you hear them?

:: Getting There

From Keystone Heights, drive north on FL 21 for 6 miles. Gold Head Branch State Park will be on your right.

GPS COORDINATES   N29° 49' 48.9" W81° 57' 1.0"

20

Hammock Campground at Jennings State Forest

The tent sites here are private, shady, and make for an ideal basecamp to hike, pedal, and paddle Jennings State Forest.

Jennings State Forest stretches across 23,000 acres of fast-growing northern Clay County as well as a portion of Duval County, near the town of Middleburg. Centered on North Fork Black Creek, the forest provides recreational opportunities for visitors, a place for wildlife to call home, and an oasis of preserved natural communities vital to northeast Florida's long-term vigor.

Hammock Campground is stretched along a narrow dirt-and-sand track that loops through a gorgeous woodland of live oak, laurel oak, and pine, with scattered palmetto and brush. The 10 campsites—all finely shaded—are spaced well apart along the loop road. Campsite 1 is just past the pay station/kiosk, set in deep woods. The

next few campsites sit along both sides of the rustic road and are so well separated you can hardly see from one campsite to the next. Campsite 5 is large. Just beyond there, reach a small pavilion with a nearby group fire ring. This shelter would come in handy during a rainy day. Campsite 6 is just across from the pavilion. The vault toilet is off to the right of here in the woods. The last four sites are strung out under oaks, and all have excellent privacy. If only all campgrounds were laid out this way!

Make sure to bring your own drinking water. This campground rarely fills. Fall through spring is the time to set up your tent then explore the outdoor offerings of Jennings State Forest. Before you arrive, download a map of the forest—it'll be much easier to execute your adventures.

Hiking is a winner here. You pass two major trailheads en route to the campground. Take the North Fork Black Creek Trail for a 5.2-mile loop through the hills, woods, and streams of Jennings State Forest. First, travel along and across Sweetwater Branch before finding North Fork Black Creek. The last part

:: Ratings

BEAUTY: ★ ★ ★ ★
PRIVACY: ★ ★ ★ ★ ★
SPACIOUSNESS: ★ ★ ★ ★
QUIET: ★ ★ ★ ★
SECURITY: ★ ★
CLEANLINESS: ★ ★ ★

:: Key Information

ADDRESS: 1337 Long Horn Road Middleburg, FL 32068	**FACILITIES:** Vault toilet
OPERATED BY: Florida Forest Service	**PARKING:** At campsites only
CONTACT: 904-291-5530; freshfromflorida.com	**FEE:** $10 per night
	ELEVATION: 80'
OPEN: Year-round	
SITES: 10	**RESTRICTIONS:**
	■ **Pets:** On leash only
EACH SITE: Picnic table, fire ring, tent pad, auto pad	■ **Fires:** In fire rings only
	■ **Alcohol:** Prohibited
ASSIGNMENT: First come, first served; no reservation	■ **Vehicles:** Must park on gravel parking pads
REGISTRATION: At entrance station	■ **Other:** No generators at campsites

of the loop takes you over rolling terrain and through pine flatwoods. Dawn or dusk hikers stand a decent chance of seeing deer, turkey, or maybe even a passing bear. The Fire and Water Nature Trail makes a 1.8-mile circuit. This trail travels dry hills and moist lower areas while visiting a mosaic of plant communities. Enjoy the informative stops that explain the importance of fire and water for Florida's woodlands. Peer out from a wildlife blind and enjoy an overlook along Wheeler Branch while looking for insect-eating pitcher plants.

Paddlers will love floating North Fork Black Creek. I recommend the 5-mile run from Ellis Ford to Indian Ford. The put-in and takeout are accessible by two-wheel vehicles with decent clearance. The wilderness feel is palpable—and surprising—considering the proximity to Jacksonville. The "real Florida" banks complement the tea-colored stream as it swiftly bends around innumerable curves bordered by high banks. Interestingly, you will pass a few simple yet exciting rapids. Look for rock outcrops in the water here, and plan to dodge around a few fallen trees. Indian Ford is the last takeout in the state forest. The USGS gauge is North Fork Black Creek near Middleburg, Florida. The discharge should be a minimum of 60 cubic feet per second. It is advisable to call the state forest for the latest paddling conditions. Bicycles can tool along the sand roads of the forest. So even though Hammock Campground is scenic, the forest activities will draw you away from your shady site here at Jennings State Forest.

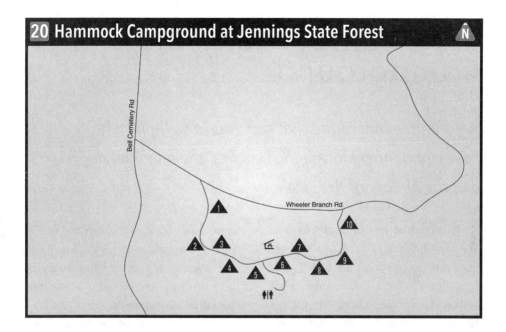

:: Getting There

From Exit 12 on I-295 southwest of downtown Jacksonville, take Blanding Boulevard, FL 21, south 8 miles to Old Jennings Road. Turn right onto Old Jennings Road and follow it 4.1 miles nearly to a dead end, then turn right on Live Oak Lane, a sand road. Follow it 2.7 miles, then turn on primitive Bell Cemetery Road. Follow Bell Cemetery Road 1.4 miles, then turn left on Wheeler Branch Road and follow it 0.1 mile, then reach the campground on your right.

GPS COORDINATES   N 30° 8' 47.3" W 81°54' 40.2"

21

Little Talbot Island State Park Campground

A 40-unit campground that serves as a well-placed base camp for exploring the beaches, the marshlands, and the history of the locale.

Little Talbot Island State Park is one of the area parks collectively known as the Talbot Islands State Parks. In addition to Little Talbot, there is Big Talbot Island, Long Island, Fort George Island, and Amelia Island State Park. Little Talbot has a 40-unit campground that serves as a well-placed base camp for exploring the beaches, the marshlands, and the history of the locale.

The campground is across FL A1A from the ocean and backs up to a salt marsh. The forest here is fairly thick, a mixture of slash pine, live oak, red cedar, southern magnolia, and palm. An understory of American holly, saw palmetto, and yaupon (another type of holly)

provides fine campsite buffers and breaks up the campground. Be aware that the 40 campsites are not uniform in size. Check out the campsites to find a site to suit your dimensional needs.

The campground is divided into three loops of hard, packed lime rock with a spur road leading to each loop. Campsites are located along the spur roads as well as the loops themselves. There are no campsites on the insides of the loops. The first loop has nine campsites, mostly on the spur road. A short, dead-end road holds two sites.

The central loop has 13 sites. Most of these are on the spur road too. The canopy is a little more open here, with more slash pines. Its proximity to the low-lying salt marsh allows more light. A small playground sits in the center of this loop.

The third loop has the longest spur road and 18 campsites. Those along the road sit across from an ancient sand dune that is now forested. Some of the campsites on the loop open up to the salt

:: Ratings

BEAUTY: ★ ★ ★ ★
PRIVACY: ★ ★ ★
SPACIOUSNESS: ★ ★ ★
QUIET: ★ ★ ★
SECURITY: ★ ★ ★ ★ ★
CLEANLINESS: ★ ★ ★ ★

:: Key Information

ADDRESS: Little Talbot Island State Park, 12157 Heckscher Dr. Jacksonville, FL 32226

OPERATED BY: Florida State Parks

CONTACT: 904-251-2320, floridastate parks.org; reservations 800-326-3521, reserveamerica.com

OPEN: Year-round

SITES: 40

EACH SITE: Picnic table, fire ring, water spigot, electricity

ASSIGNMENT: Online or by ranger

REGISTRATION: By phone or at park entrance booth

FACILITIES: Hot showers, flush toilets, laundry

PARKING: At campsites only

FEE: $24/night

ELEVATION: Sea level

RESTRICTIONS:

- **Pets:** On 6-foot leash maximum
- **Fires:** In fire rings only
- **Alcohol:** Prohibited
- **Vehicles:** None
- **Other:** 14-day stay limit

marsh and, consequently, have the best views in the campground.

A campground gate keeps the area safe and secure. Two bathhouses are well situated and close to all campers. Both have hot showers and flush toilets. A washer and dryer are located at both south and north bathhouses.

Across the road, Little Talbot Island has more than 5 miles of pristine beach. Sunbathe, surf-cast, or just watch the waves roll in. Don't be surprised to see surfers riding the waves out on North Point. If you are in a walking mood, you can take the Island Hiking Trail to the beach. It starts near the park entrance station and travels through varying maritime plant communities to access the beach at 2.4 miles. Then 1.7 miles of beach walking will return you to the first

boardwalk that crosses the dunes back to the main campground road.

The marsh side of the island is worth a look too. A 1-mile nature trail leaves directly from the campground and skirts the tidal estuary where anglers are often seen casting for redfish and sea trout. The marsh is also great for crabbing.

Fort George Island has an informative 4-mile trail of its own. The Saturiwa Trail tells the history of man and the island over the last 5,000 years. You also get to climb Mount Cornelia, the highest coastal point between here and North Carolina. It is an ancient dune that allows views of the mouth of the St. Johns River.

Big Talbot Island is a little more on the quiet side. It is another sea island that offers canoeing, fishing, hiking, and sunbathing. There is a spot known as the

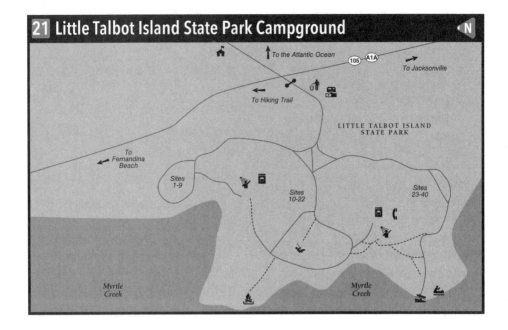

Bluffs that sports a view of Nassau Sound and is a popular photography spot. Nature lovers will really enjoy this island.

Amelia Island is next up the chain of sea islands. The state park is the only undeveloped part of Amelia Island. The highlight here is the opportunity to rent horses and saddle up for a ride along the beach—a very rare opportunity in this day and age.

The Talbot Islands State Parks offer a wide variety of recreational situations. The campground on Little Talbot Island makes an attractive and safe base camp to see the sea islands of northern Florida.

:: Getting There

From I-95 in Jacksonville, take FL 105 north (Heckscher Drive) 22 miles to Little Talbot Island State Park, which will be on your right. Be aware that after 20 miles, FL 105 turns into FL A1A.

GPS COORDINATES   N30° 26' 46.0" W81° 24' 58.7"

22

Manatee Springs State Park Campground

The combination of the historic Suwannee River, a huge spring, varied plant communities, and a mammal reserve make Manatee Springs an easy choice.

When the state of Florida began planning state parks, Manatee Springs was one of the first places that came to mind. No wonder—the combination of the historic Suwannee River, a huge spring, varied plant communities, and a mammal reserve make Manatee Springs an easy choice. And with a non-electric camping loop, your choice to come here should be just as easy.

The 86-site campground is divided into three loops. The Magnolia 2 camping area has the largest sites. This spells *RVs*. The tall canopy of hardwood has some of the 14 species of oak that thrive in this park, as well as mockernut hickory and butternut hickory. The understory

:: Ratings

BEAUTY: ★ ★ ★
PRIVACY: ★ ★ ★
SPACIOUSNESS: ★ ★ ★
QUIET: ★ ★ ★ ★
SECURITY: ★ ★ ★ ★ ★
CLEANLINESS: ★ ★ ★ ★

of red bay and palmetto provides some campsite buffers. A children's play area and a fully equipped comfort station are located here. Sand and leaves cover the Magnolia 2 loop. Stay here only if the other two loops are full.

The Hickory loop is more isolated, with a primarily hardwood forest, but with a thicker understory of primarily magnolia and red bay.

Magnolia 1 is the best. There is a mixed forest of evergreen and deciduous trees with the thickest understory of the loops. It is mostly sparkleberry, red bay, and smaller trees. This camping area has an unusual loop-within-a-loop configuration.

The outer loop has sites that are nestled into their own wooded cubby-holes. Some campsites have tent pads; all campsites have a lantern post. Campsite buffers divide the sites, most of which are located on the outside of the loop.

The inner loop has been converted to walk-in tent sites, which we tent campers love. These sites are closest to the bathhouse, also. The Magnolia 1 loop is almost

:: Key Information

ADDRESS: Manatee Springs State Park
11650 NW 115th Street
Chiefland, FL 32626

OPERATED BY: Florida State Parks

CONTACT: 352-493-6072, floridastate
parks.org; reservations 800-326-3521,
reserveamerica.com

OPEN: Year-round

SITES: 86

EACH SITE: Picnic tables, fire ring,
water, electricity

ASSIGNMENT: Online or by ranger

REGISTRATION: By phone or at park
entrance booth

FACILITIES: Hot showers, flush toilets

PARKING: At campsites only

FEE: $20/night

ELEVATION: 30'

RESTRICTIONS:

■ **Pets:** On 6-foot leash
■ **Fires:** In fire rings only
■ **Alcohol:** Prohibited
■ **Vehicles:** 2 vehicles/site

exclusively occupied by tent campers. It
is also the most attractive camping area,
and the one I recommend.

Manatee Springs impresses as well.
It boils up more than 80,000 gallons of
clear water per minute. A viewing path
lies all around the springhead, where you
can look into the water and see lots of
fish, turtles, and other aquatic life. Just
below the spring's beginning is a roped-
off swimming area. Be warned that this
swimming area is in the current of Manatee Spring's short but swift flow to the
Suwannee River. A calmer pool area has
been built across the spring and is accessible by a short foot trail.

Below the swimming area is the
canoe launch. Kayaks, pedal boats,
and canoes can be rented, and you can
paddle to the Suwannee. Summer will
find tubers floating down the spring and
then walking back up time and again

via a short boardwalk that meanders
through a cypress swamp bordering the
spring run.

Viewing platforms have been erected
for peering out into the water to look for
manatees. At the end of the boardwalk is
a dock for boaters, anglers, and manatee
watchers. Here I saw manatees swimming just inside the warmth of the spring
run, facing upstream and coming up for
air every few minutes.

The North End Trail System is a
collection of old fire roads that crisscross the park property for a collective
8.5 miles. These trails pass all manner
of forest communities that inhabit this
river valley. Both walkers and bicyclers
are welcome to enjoy the forest. Tur-
keys, deer, foxes, and wild boars call this
woodland home.

The North End Nature Walk uses
some of the trails for an interpretive walk

22 Manatee Springs State Park Campground

that employs a handheld guide and numbered posts. Learn about the plants and trees of this forest and how they interact with each other. Shacklefoot Pond and Graveyard Pond are two worthwhile destinations in the system's northeastern end. Three other trails end near the Suwannee River. Get a map at the ranger station so that you don't end up walking in circles.

The great naturalist William Bartram lauded the natural beauty of this area. The state of Florida had Manatee Springs on its short list of initial state parks. Put Manatee Springs on your short list of Florida treasures to come and visit.

:: Getting There

From Chiefland, drive west on FL 320 for 6 miles. Manatee Springs State Park will be straight ahead.

GPS COORDINATES   N29° 29' 22.0" W82° 58' 26.3"

23

O'Leno State Park Campground

O'Leno can be a fun family getaway or a quiet off-season retreat.

O'Leno State Park has a strange name derivation. First, there was the town of Keno, which was founded near where the Santa Fe River sinks into the limestone below. Keno is a card game of chance, so the town's religious folk decided to rename the town to Leno, to save its reputation. Leno soon disappeared after the railroad passed it by. People referred to the area as "ol' Leno," thus the name for the park, O'Leno.

The Santa Fe River was the reason for the town, and now the river is the reason for the park. The area between the river sink and river rise has been a major crossing point for as long as man has been around. Many who crossed camped in the area; now you can too. The two park campgrounds, Dogwood and Magnolia, serve tent campers well.

Dogwood Campground is located near the park entrance. A hard, packed-sand road leads into a now-forested sink-hole. The large loop is in a forest of many hardwoods: laurel oak, pignut hickory, and mockernut hickory. Dogwood trees form part of the understory, which also includes many brier patches—nobody wants to walk through them.

The loop rises as it circles around. The campsites are large and well spaced. Brier-free paths lead to the comfort station in the center of the loop. Its distance from the rest of the park makes it the most isolated loop. If the camping is really slow, this loop may be closed.

Magnolia Campground is located on more level ground. It was built when the park was founded. Loblolly pines tower overhead, along with laurel oak and a few other hardwoods. An understory of red cedar, holly, and, of course, magnolia fills the forest.

The more elongated Magnolia loop has large and open campsites. One small

:: Ratings

BEAUTY: ★ ★ ★
PRIVACY: ★ ★ ★
SPACIOUSNESS: ★ ★ ★
QUIET: ★ ★ ★
SECURITY: ★ ★ ★ ★ ★
CLEANLINESS: ★ ★ ★ ★

:: Key Information

ADDRESS: O'Leno State Park
410 SE O'Leno Park Road
High Springs, FL 32643

OPERATED BY: Florida State Parks

CONTACT: 386-454-1853, floridastate
parks.org; reservations 800-326-3521,
reserveamerica.com

OPEN: Year-round

SITES: 61

EACH SITE: Picnic table, fire ring,
water, electricity

ASSIGNMENT: Online or by ranger

REGISTRATION: By phone or at park
entrance booth

FACILITIES: Hot showers, flush toilets

PARKING: At campsites only

FEE: $18/night

ELEVATION: 70'

RESTRICTIONS:

■ **Pets:** On 6-foot leash only

■ **Fires:** In fire rings only

■ **Alcohol:** Prohibited

■ **Vehicles:** 2 vehicles/site

■ **Other:** 30-day stay limit

road bisects the loop but has no camp-sites on it. All the sites are on the outside of the loop. A comfort station rests in the loop center.

Both campgrounds are attractive. Magnolia may lure more RVs. Summer weekends are busy for O'Leno. Winter can be very quiet but is a good time to hike many of the excellent park trails. The Dogwood Trail leads from Dogwood Campground to the Santa Fe River area, center for most of the park's recreation.

The mile-long River Trail crosses the Santa Fe and heads upstream before looping around to circle the river sink, the spot where the river follows subter-ranean passageways to emerge above-ground later. The 1.5-mile River Rise Trail leads from the gate on US 441 and goes to

the spot where the Santa Fe emerges from the ground to flow again.

Hikers and bikers can both use the Pareners Branch Loop. It passes its stream namesake and goes by some sinks, areas where the limestone has given way, forming a hole in the ground. Part of the trail follows the historic Wire Road that passed this way to cross the Santa Fe where it flowed underground. The Lime-stone Trail starts on the main park road. It travels by numerous rock outcrops and through a hardwood hammock on its half-mile loop. An additional 35 miles of hiking/biking/equestrian trails can be found at adjacent River Rise Preserve State Park.

The Santa Fe River is popular for swimming. Near the footbridge is a

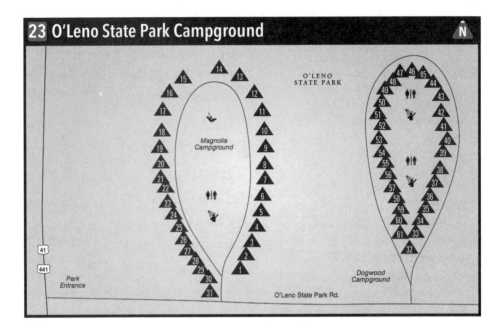

roped-off area with concrete steps leading down to water. Canoes are for rent at the park to explore the scenic river, but fishing is said to be unpredictable.

Many O'Leno campers drive to nearby Ichetucknee Springs State Park. The springs here put forth 233 million gallons of water a day. Tubers love to float the clear water in the summertime. These springs are a National Natural Landmark.

It's hard to believe a town once was at O'Leno State Park. O'Leno can be a fun family getaway or a quiet off-season retreat. Many have passed this way across the Santa Fe River by way of land. Make sure you pass this way too.

:: Getting There

From High Springs, drive north on US 441 for 6 miles. O'Leno State Park will be on your right.

GPS COORDINATES   N29° 54' 51.5" W82° 36' 29.8"

24

Ocean Pond Campground

An appealing campground in the diverse
Osceola National Forest

Ocean Pond is a misleading name for the body of water by this campground. Neither ocean nor pond, it is a bowl-shaped lake 2 miles in diameter. It is not, however, misleading to call this Forest Service recreation area scenic and worth a visit.

The campground is spread along the shore of Ocean Pond. Tall pines tower overhead. Spanish moss hangs from the hardwoods. A dense understory of palmetto and young oak thrives where it hasn't been cut back. Grass and pine needles carpet the forest edges. Cypress trees border Ocean Pond.

Just beyond the registration board are the only two marginal sites. They are open and too close to the road. Just beyond these two sites, the main campground road divides. To the right is a large

:: Ratings

BEAUTY: ★ ★ ★ ★
PRIVACY: ★ ★ ★ ★
SPACIOUSNESS: ★ ★ ★ ★
QUIET: ★ ★
SECURITY: ★ ★ ★
CLEANLINESS: ★ ★ ★ ★

loop containing only seven sites. The campground host shares this loop, which is set back from the lake. These sites are very roomy and relaxed, seeming to form a separate mini-campground. A bathhouse with a hot shower serves this loop.

To the left is the bulk of the campground. A sandy road stretches along the shore. Seven of the coveted lakeside sites sit on one side of the road. Here, you can float your boat right up to the campsite. Across from the main road is a spur road containing large sites by a comfort station.

Farther on is a mini loop that includes three more lakeside sites. These sites are large as well, with their own comfort station. A final loop contains the 20 remaining sites. Five open sites and a comfort station occupy the interior of the loop. Three more sites are directly lakeside. The rest are cut into the thick woods, offering the maximum in site privacy, though they may be a bit buggy on a still summer day.

Overall, the campsites are among the largest I've ever seen. Plenty of brush provides more than ample site privacy, though the lakeside sites are more open. Water spigots are spread throughout the campground. RVs will head to the 19

:: Key Information

<table>
<tr><td>

ADDRESS: Ocean Pond Campground
US 90 East, P.O. Box 70
Olustee, FL 32072

OPERATED BY: US Forest Service

CONTACT: 386-752-2577,
www.fs.usda.gov/osceola

OPEN: Year-round

SITES: 67

EACH SITE: Tent pad, picnic table, fire
ring, lantern post, some have water
and electricity

ASSIGNMENT: First come, first served

REGISTRATION: Self-registration on-site

</td><td>

FACILITIES: Hot showers, flush toilets

PARKING: At campsites only

FEE: $6 primitive, $12 water sites,
$18 electric sites

ELEVATION: 160'

RESTRICTIONS:

■ **Pets:** On leash only, must be kept
out of beach area

■ **Fires:** In fire rings only

■ **Vehicles:** None

■ **Other:** 14-day stay limit

</td></tr>
</table>

electric sites. A drawback is that when the wind blows the wrong way, you can sometimes hear traffic from I-10.

Ocean Pond attracts a cross section of campers who enjoy a cross section of activities. It is full on summer weekends and holidays but maintains a pleasant atmosphere. The ultimate testimony comes from the campground host. This is a coveted job for which retirees vie. Get here early during this time, as it is first come, first served.

A boat ramp serves the campground, allowing boaters to fish for largemouth bass, bluegill, or crappie. Ocean Pond is big enough to enjoy other water sports too. Both kids and adults can enjoy the campground swimming beach. Near the beach is a grassy glade ideal for sunbathing, throwing a Frisbee, or just relaxing on the lakefront benches.

Ocean Pond is lucky enough to be in the path of the state's most famous walkway, the Florida National Scenic Trail. A 22-mile stretch of the trail winds northwest through the Osceola National Forest, from Olustee Battlefield to US 441. You can traverse one of the more than 20 boardwalks that span swamps and other wetlands of the north Florida flatwoods. I've walked the entire 1,100-mile Florida Trail and consider this one of the best segments of the path.

The Olustee Battlefield is just a short drive or a longer walk from Ocean Pond. Here is the site of the battle of Olustee, the largest Civil War battle fought in Florida. Explore the small museum there.

Numerous lakes, creeks, and ponds are sprinkled about the Osceola. But the most interesting feature may be the

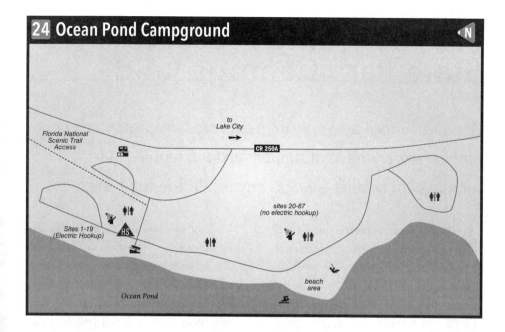

24 Ocean Pond Campground

to Lake City

Florida National Scenic Trail Access

CR 250A

sites 20-67 (no electric hookup)

Sites 1-19 (Electric Hookup)

HS

beach area

Ocean Pond

13,600-acre Big Gum Swamp Wilderness. The water table is generally near the surface, creating a spongy mat that may or may not hold you up. Piney woods and sluggish creeks add to the terrain. One trail, the Silver Dot, starts near Forest Route 262. The adventurous can follow old elevated tramways, remnants of "turpentining" operations of the late 1800s. Be sure to stop at the Osceola District Office between Lake City and Ocean Pond for a detailed map.

No matter where you go in the Osceola National Forest, make Ocean Pond your base camp. It is an appealing campground in a diverse national forest.

:: Getting There

From Lake City, drive east on US 90 for 14 miles. Turn left at County Road 250A just beyond the town of Olustee. Follow CR 250A for 4 miles, and turn left into the campground entrance.

GPS COORDINATES   N30° 13' 50.8" W82° 24' 49.5"

25

Paynes Prairie Preserve State Park Campground

A well-arranged tent-only area—located in more than 20,000 acres of water and land supporting bird, reptile, and mammalian wildlife—makes Paynes Prairie complete.

A **buffalo on** a prairie was about the last thing I expected to see in Florida. But there it was. After perusing the area, I understood why Florida designated Paynes Prairie a preserve. More than 20,000 acres of water and land support bird, reptile, and mammalian wildlife. The well-arranged tent-only area completes the Paynes Prairie package.

It's not a prairie in the midwestern sense, but rather a basin of grassy marshland surrounded by forest. The vegetation that grows on the prairie gives a sense of endless grassland. The grass and forest are constantly giving and taking as the water rises and lowers. It is a story of nature that has to be seen to be appreciated.

:: Ratings

BEAUTY: ★ ★ ★
PRIVACY: ★ ★ ★ ★
SPACIOUSNESS: ★ ★ ★
QUIET: ★ ★
SECURITY: ★ ★ ★ ★ ★
CLEANLINESS: ★ ★ ★ ★

Tent campers can surely appreciate the campground. It rests in a mixed forest of pine, laurel oak, and hardwoods, such as maple. Younger hardwood seedlings and some palmetto form an adequate understory. Magnolia and holly are also present. The woods are certainly pleasing to the eye.

The campground is arranged in a loop. The first 18 campsites are for all types of campers, and some sites have built-in tent pads. Just beyond the foot trail to Lake Wauberg, the tent-camping area begins. Four parking areas are there for tent campers to pull in; then it's a short walk to their sites, nestled in the woods. Electrical hookups are randomly spread about the tent area. Not all tenters can access these plugs, unless they bring a very long extension cord.

Campsites 19–22 have their own little walking loop. They are closest to Lake Wauberg but don't access it. The next three sites, 23–25, have their own loop. One of the campsites is close to the road, and the other two are back 30–40 yards.

:: Key Information

ADDRESS: Paynes Prairie Preserve State Park, 100 Savannah Blvd. Micanopy, FL 32667

OPERATED BY: Florida State Parks

CONTACT: 352-466-3397, floridastate parks.org; reservations 800-326-3521, reserveamerica.com

OPEN: Year-round

SITES: 15 tent only, 35 tent and RV

EACH SITE: Picnic table, fire ring, water, lantern post, electricity

ASSIGNMENT: Online or assigned by ranger

REGISTRATION: Online or at park entrance booth

FACILITIES: Hot showers, flush toilets

PARKING: At campsites and overflow parking

FEE: $18/night

ELEVATION: 75'

RESTRICTIONS:

- **Pets:** Prohibited
- **Fires:** In fire rings only
- **Alcohol:** Prohibited
- **Vehicles:** None

These sites have the best privacy, though all the tent-camping sites have ample privacy and spaciousness.

The next eight campsites are mostly back off the road and are connected to two parking areas by paths. Pine needles cover the ground here. The woods and the distance from the road make for a wonderful tent-camping experience here. The only drawback is the low hum of autos from I-75 a few miles away.

The main camping loop continues with 17 sites. These campsites are all appealing and attractive, but the tent sites are the only way to go at Paynes Prairie. Two bathhouses serve the campground. They both have hot showers and flush toilets.

I methodically explored this large preserve. First, I watched the 20-minute video in the visitor center to grasp an overall perspective. I highly recommend the video. There are places it shows that you simply can't access by trail. Then I climbed the observation tower overlooking the prairie. I spotted two of the wild horses and a buffalo. I returned to camp after watching the sun set over Lake Wauberg. Back at my campsite, I perused the preserve map for the next day's hiking opportunities.

There are plenty. Cone's Dike is an 8-mile round-trip jaunt that heads into the marsh. Chacala is a series of loops that starts near the campground, encompassing varied terrain and eventually reaching Chacala Pond. Both of these trails are for hikers and bikers. Bolen's Bluff Trail starts off US 441, travels 1.5 miles into the marsh, and ends

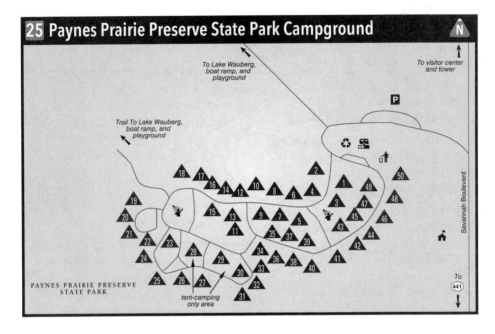

25 Paynes Prairie Preserve State Park Campground

at a wildlife viewing deck. The 17-mile Gainesville–Hawthorne Trail is a Rails-to-Trails project that is open to horses as well as to hikers and bikers.

Lake Wauberg makes an ideal paddling destination, whether or not you are fishing. Gas-powered engines are prohibited, making for a quiet kayaking or canoeing experience. Keep an eye open for alligators. Nearby Gainesville offers the eclectic atmosphere of a university town. Watch for gators here too.

Humans have been a presence on the prairie for thousands of years. Thankfully, the state is restoring and making Paynes Prairie available for both wildlife and humans to range and roam upon. You have got to see it to truly appreciate it.

:: Getting There

From Gainesville, drive south on US 441 about 10 miles. Paynes Prairie Preserve State Park will be to the west.

GPS COORDINATES   N29° 32' 38.2" W82° 17' 49.7"

26

Suwannee River State Park Campground

Suwannee River State Park has a good campground. It has better nature trails. And it has Florida's greatest river.

This park is a good example of a state protecting, developing, and preserving a special area for present and future generations to enjoy. At this site, the town of Columbus once saw steamboats coming and going along the Suwannee River. The city eventually was abandoned. Confederate soldiers once protected this important river; you can still see their earthworks. Today, forest has reclaimed the area. The Suwannee and its tributary the Withlacoochee—which enters the Suwannee at the state park— are equally important for their scenic value, as they have always been. The state of Florida rightly saw fit to make this one of its first state parks, starting with 300 acres in 1936 and expanding to more than 1,800 acres today.

:: Ratings

BEAUTY: ★ ★ ★
PRIVACY: ★ ★ ★
SPACIOUSNESS: ★ ★ ★ ★
QUIET: ★ ★ ★ ★
SECURITY: ★ ★ ★ ★
CLEANLINESS: ★ ★ ★ ★

The Suwannacoochee Camp Area is located on a high area back from the Suwannee River. Follow the paved road through the campground. Tall laurel oak, live oak, and longleaf pines shade the area. There are campsites on both sides of the loop. They are large and well separated from one another but have a moderate understory of younger hardwoods.

The campground road turns left just before coming to the historic stagecoach road that once ran through Columbus. The forest floor is thick with oak leaves and pine needles. As the campground road turns away from the stagecoach road, all the campsites are on the inside of the loop. Holly trees and vines complement the understory. Across from these sites is a field, which offers more light than the forested area. It may be a good idea to camp at these sites on a dark day.

As the campground road makes its final turn, two more campsites appear on the outside of the loop. These sites are the largest in the campground.

The comfort station with hot showers and flush toilets is in the loop's center.

:: Key Information

ADDRESS: Suwannee River State Park
3631 201st Path
Live Oak, FL 32060

OPERATED BY: Florida State Parks

CONTACT: 386-362-2746, floridastate
parks.org; reservations 800-326-3521,
reserveamerica.com

OPEN: Year-round

SITES: 30

EACH SITE: Picnic table, fire ring,
water, electricity, sewer

ASSIGNMENT: Online and first come,
first served

REGISTRATION: Online and at ranger
station at 5 p.m. in winter, 6 p.m. in
summer

FACILITIES: Showers, flush toilets,
laundry

PARKING: At campsites and extra car
parking

FEE: $22/night

ELEVATION: 50'

RESTRICTIONS:

■ **Pets:** On 6-foot leash maximum;
proof of vaccination required

■ **Fires:** In fire rings

■ **Alcohol:** Prohibited

■ **Vehicles:** None

■ **Other:** 14-day stay limit

It also has a washer and dryer for those dirty duds. Each campsite has posts embedded into its perimeter, marking off the sites and adding some decorative landscaping.

Every one of the 30 sites in the campground has water, electrical hook-ups, and sewers, which could result in an RV for a neighbor. The warm season sees mostly tent campers. Weekends are infrequently full, and weekdays are quiet year-round. Sometimes it's so quiet it becomes hard to imagine the town of Columbus ever being here. Suwannee River does see a fair share of travelers looking for a place to stay for the night because of its proximity to I-10 and I-75. However, on my weekday visit,

I was the only camper other than the campground host.

The Suwannee River was running even darker than normal—it was above flood stage. (The river's name derives from the Timucuan Indian word for "black water.") A light drizzle fell, and the dark sky made spring's brilliant greenery even more vivid as I hiked the series of nature trails near the campground.

I started with the Suwannee River Trail that runs along the flowing watercourse. Two other trails spur off this one. The Balanced Rock Trail heads upstream for half a mile to the Balanced Rock and connects to the Lime Sink Run Trail. It follows up a stream branch to a spring and leads back to the campground.

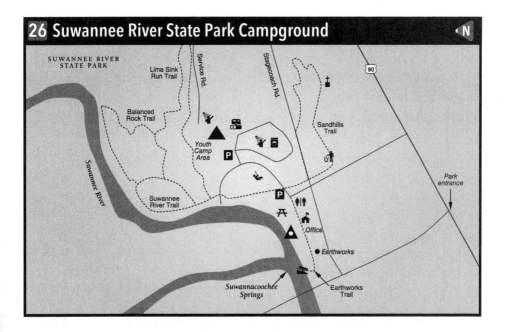

26 Suwannee River State Park Campground

There are many springs along the Suwannee and Withlacoochee Rivers, which add their waters to the Suwannee at the state park. The Earthworks Trail passes by the old mill site and the Confederate earthworks that once protected the bridge spanning the Suwannee. This trail ends at an overlook where you can see the Suwannacoochee Springs. The name reflects the confluence of the Suwannee and Withlacoochee Rivers.

The Sandhills Trail makes a 0.75-mile loop through an open, drier environment and passes the Columbus Cemetery. A fairly recent acquisition of land across the Suwannee has an 11-mile loop trail for hardy hikers that parallels the Withlacoochee River and intersects the famed Florida National Scenic Trail.

Most people rightly associate the park with canoeing. The Suwannee is Florida's greatest river; it's even mentioned in the state song. The Withlacoochee River is characterized by high limestone banks and many cypress and tupelo trees. The beautiful pool of Blue Spring is just below the put-in for a canoe run that ends at the state park.

Suwannee River State Park has a good campground. It has better nature trails. And it has Florida's greatest river. It makes for a good stopover if you are just passing through, but it also makes a fine destination in and of itself. The state was right for making Suwannee River one of its first state parks.

:: Getting There

From Live Oak, take US 90 West 11 miles. Suwannee River State Park will be on your right.

GPS COORDINATES   N30° 24' 2.9" W83° 10' 1.9"

Central Florida

27

Alexander Springs Recreation Area Campground

An upwelling of clear-blue water that rises out of the earth and instantaneously forms its own waterway: this is Alexander Springs.

Alexander Springs is clearly worth preserving—an oasis in the forest and one of the outstanding physical features of central Florida. Imagine thrashing through broken woods and coming upon an upwelling of clear-blue water that rises out of the earth and instantaneously forms its own waterway: this is Alexander Springs.

The US Forest Service recognized this aquatic wonder and built a fine recreation area around the spring. It's showing signs of age, but any man-made facility will fail to match the natural ones here. Native Timucuan Indians recognized the beauty of the springs. Their artifacts

make it evident they called it home. Now you can make the springs your home for a night or two weeks.

The campground is split into four spur roads that turn away from, then return to, the main campground road. The campground rises as it extends away from the springs. Loop A is on the highest ground, in a forest of pines with an adequate understory of palmetto. This 14-campsite loop has a central comfort station with flush toilets only. During the winter months Loop A is where the RV-driving snowbirds congregate.

Loop B spurs off to the right of the main campground road. It is more thickly forested with live oak and has a more swampy appearance, being on lower, wetter ground. The campground host resides in this loop. Warm-water showers and flush toilets are at the center of this loop in the comfort station—the only showers actually in the campground. The only other showers are located at the comfort station by the springs.

:: Ratings

BEAUTY: ★ ★ ★ ★
PRIVACY: ★ ★ ★
SPACIOUSNESS: ★ ★ ★ ★
QUIET: ★ ★ ★
SECURITY: ★ ★ ★ ★
CLEANLINESS: ★ ★ ★

:: Key Information

ADDRESS: Alexander Springs Recreation Area
17147 East FL 40
Silver Springs, FL 34488

OPERATED BY: US Forest Service

CONTACT: 352-669-3522,
www.fs.usda.gov/ocala;
reservations 877-444-6777,
recreation.gov

OPEN: Year-round

SITES: 67

EACH SITE: Picnic table, fire ring, lantern post

ASSIGNMENT: First come, first served; and by reservation

REGISTRATION: At campground entrance booth

FACILITIES: Showers, flush toilets, water spigots

PARKING: At campsites only

FEE: $21/night

ELEVATION: 55'

RESTRICTIONS:

- **Pets:** On 6-foot leash maximum
- **Fires:** In fire rings only
- **Alcohol:** At campsites only
- **Vehicles:** None
- **Other:** 14-day stay limit

Loop C is on the high side of the campground. It sits in a forest of pine, except where the spur road comes back to the main road in a stand of live oaks. Palmetto and small trees form campsite buffers. This 17-site loop also has a central comfort station.

Loop D is at the end of the campground road and is my favorite. Live oaks drape their limbs over the campsites, providing ample shade. Palmetto and hardwood seedlings separate the sites from one another. Being in the rear of the campground, this loop receives the least amount of incidental traffic.

Generous room is given to all campsites. Time has allowed vegetation to provide site buffers throughout the campground, breaking it up and enhancing everyone's experience. There is no eyesore trash here, only natural beauty.

The first thing to do is explore the springs. A picnic area leads to a swimming beach adjacent to the springs. Swimmers, snorkelers, scuba divers, and sunbathers congregate at the spot where the clear water rises from the ground and then forms its own river.

This is where the Alexander Springs Creek canoe run begins. Rent a canoe and paddle the wide, sun-splashed waterway. The current is moderate enough for you to return upstream to conclude your paddle. Or you can paddle downstream to one of three landings. You might want to bring your pole and try to catch some fish. A Florida freshwater license is required. A paddle into the Alexander Springs Wilderness from the Forest Route 52 landing to the St. Johns River is a tough but superlatively scenic 11.2-mile there-and-back paddle.

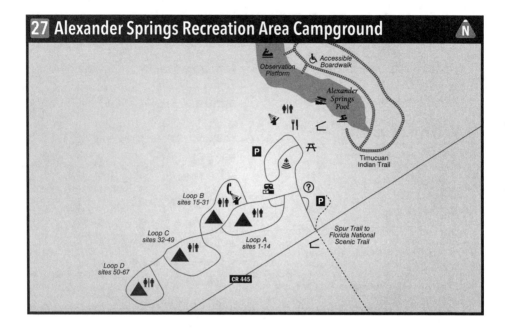

27 Alexander Springs Recreation Area Campground

For land lovers, there is the interesting 1-mile interpretive Timucuan Indian Trail. It runs near Alexander Springs and points out native plants that were used by the Indians in their everyday lives. The trail forms a loop and returns to the picnic area. A spur trail starts near the entrance booth and leads a short distance to the Florida National Scenic Trail. No matter whether you head east or west, you will see a fast-disappearing real Florida.

Hard-core natural enthusiasts will want to explore the Billies Bay Wilderness, which surrounds Alexander Springs on three sides. The centerpiece of this wilderness is Nine Mile Creek. Make sure to talk to a ranger or an experienced local before you delve into this primitive section of the Ocala National Forest. Alexander Springs is a year-round attraction and will be busy on summer and winter weekends. So whether you come here to cool off from the heat or cool down from the stresses of everyday life, your needs will be met.

:: Getting There

From Umatilla, go north on FL 19 for 8 miles. Turn right on County Road 445 and drive 5 miles. Alexander Springs Recreation Area will be on your left.

GPS COORDINATES   N29° 4' 48.4" W81° 34' 38.5"

28

Blue Spring State Park Campground

The springs keep the endangered manatee warm in the winter and you cool in the summer.

Every winter, manatees leave the cooling waters of the St. Johns River to make the tepid 72°F waters of Blue Spring their home. Now this park, home to Blue Spring, is a designated manatee refuge and is a wonderful place to observe the gentle creature in winter. In the summer, human creatures flock to the spring to swim in the waters and escape the heat. As a result, the park and the campground stay fairly busy year-round.

The campground is situated atop a sandy hill in a sand-scrub thicket. A hard, packed-sand road forms a large loop with a smaller inner loop. Throughout the campground, the understory of wax myrtle and laurel oak, along with other bushes, forms dense campsite buffers, allowing the maximum in privacy but offering little overhead protection from the sun.

The campsites are bright and open overhead in the main loop, though a tree canopy forms in places, allowing some shade. This is when booking a site online can be troublesome, since you don't know which ones are shady.

Just past this group of campsites, the inner loop begins. It has six sites. This inner loop is closer to either of the comfort stations, both of which have hot showers and flush toilets for each sex. Returning to the main loop, a last grouping of seven sites brings you to the beginning of the campground.

The lack of shade may sound unappealing, but this campground is unusual for Florida. There is a hint of hilliness to it, and the dense brush between campsites is a plus for campers who value privacy. Most sites have enough growth around them to shield all but the direct rays of the noontime sun from their campsites. I suggest appreciating the privacy and bringing a tarp to screen you overhead.

:: Ratings

BEAUTY: ★ ★ ★
PRIVACY: ★ ★ ★ ★ ★
SPACIOUSNESS: ★ ★ ★
QUIET: ★ ★
SECURITY: ★ ★ ★ ★ ★
CLEANLINESS: ★ ★ ★ ★

:: Key Information

ADDRESS: Blue Spring State Park
2100 West French Ave.
Orange City, FL 32763

OPERATED BY: Florida State Parks

CONTACT: 386-775-3663, floridastate
parks.org; reservations 800-326-3521,
reserveamerica.com

OPEN: Year-round

SITES: 51

EACH SITE: Picnic table, fire grate,
water, electricity

ASSIGNMENT: Online or assigned by
ranger

REGISTRATION: Online, by phone, or
at park entrance booth

FACILITIES: Showers, flush toilets,
camp store, dump station

PARKING: At campsites only

FEE: $24/night

ELEVATION: 35'

RESTRICTIONS:

■ Pets: On 6-foot leash maximum;
proof of vaccination required

■ Fires: In fire grates only

■ Alcohol: Prohibited

■ Vehicles: Maximum length 31';
2 vehicles/site

On my trip to Blue Spring, I walked straight from the campground to the boardwalk that meanders the length of the spring from its wellhead to its confluence with the St. Johns River. I entered the shady hammock and looked out on the clear water as it flowed by. Passing the entrance point for scuba divers, I sought the springs' "boil." The area has been restored from earlier days when swimmers destroyed the springside vegetation.

There it was, the blue hole for which the area was named. Divers can reach 120 feet into the spring before the force of its upwelling turns them back. Following the flow back downstream, I came to the primary observation deck. The waters revealed a plethora of fish below me: bass, bream, catfish, and long-nosed gar.

Across the flow from the deck I spotted it—a manatee! It was facing upstream,

rising every few minutes to get a breath of air. Later, I saw a mother and calf, gliding upstream toward the springhead. This area is off-limits to all boats and serves as a protective zone for some of the approximately 85 manatees of the St. Johns River system.

Turning around, I looked over the Thursby House—built on a mound of snail shells! Snails were the primary food for the Indians of this region, and they left piles of shells as testimony to the importance of this food in their diet. This three-story house was once the center of activity in the early days of orange cultivation in central Florida.

Boaters have access to the ramp near the Thursby House, and canoes as well as kayaks are for rent too. Fishing in the St. Johns is said to be good. You can see for yourself that there are fish in the vicinity. Perhaps the best way to enjoy the water is

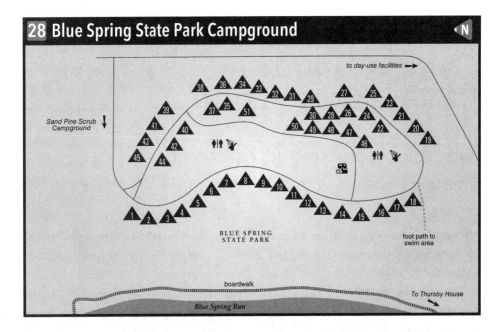

28 Blue Spring State Park Campground

to take a 2-hour ecotour of the St. Johns. Tour boats depart twice daily; riding above, you can see the wildlife of the river system below.

Hikers can take their own ecotour of the park on the 4-mile Backwoods Trail. It takes you through hardwood hammocks, marsh, cypress swamp, and pine flatwoods. Give yourself enough time to return, as this trail is a one-way trip.

No matter what the season, Blue Spring has something to offer. The springs keep the endangered manatee warm in the winter and you cool in the summer. Don't pass this central Florida attraction by for that other one in Orlando.

:: Getting There

From US 17/US 92 in Orange City, drive 2 miles west on West French Avenue to Blue Spring State Park, which will be on your left.

GPS COORDINATES   N28° 56′ 43.9″ W81° 20′ 32.3″

29

Chassahowitzka River Campground: Indian Ridge Loop

Make this your base camp for exploring the Chassahowitzka River and the adjacent wildlife refuge.

The Chassahowitzka River Campground is at the head of a spring and makes for an ideal location to explore this watery Florida treasure. The Chassahowitzka River is the centerpiece of the 32,000-acre Chassahowitzka River National Wildlife Refuge. This piece of wild Florida can be explored by water or on foot. A boat launch is within walking distance of the campground. Other pursuits in the refuge must be accessed by car first. The campground itself is owned by Citrus County and run by concessionaires. Floridians have been coming here for a long time. Decades ago it was known as Miss Maggie's. It was later bought by the Lykes Brothers, and finally by the county. Today tent campers can enjoy their own area, known as Indian Ridge, and carry on the tradition of getting away from it all on Florida's west coast.

The campground is divided into two loops. Tent campers should be primarily concerned with Indian Ridge Campground, which is a 25-site loop located in an almost tropical-looking forest of live oak, pine, palm, maple, magnolia, and laurel oaks. A healthy dose of palmetto bushes provides decent campsite privacy between most sites. Ultra-thick cypress woodland encircles the campground. Six water spigots serve the tent-camping loop. Sites 58 and 61 are very desirable, with good privacy. Site 75 is large. Some of the sites are a little close together, but early arrivers can avoid these. On your first trip, I suggest getting here during an off time to make sure you get a good campsite that may become your favorite.

:: Ratings

BEAUTY: ★ ★ ★ ★
PRIVACY: ★ ★ ★
SPACIOUSNESS: ★ ★
QUIET: ★ ★ ★
SECURITY: ★ ★ ★ ★
CLEANLINESS: ★ ★ ★ ★

:: Key Information

ADDRESS: 8600 West Miss Maggie Drive, Homosassa, FL 34448

OPERATED BY: Citrus County

CONTACT: 352-382-2200, chassahowitzkaflorida.com

OPEN: Year-round

SITES: 25 tent only, 53 other sites

EACH SITE: Tent sites have picnic tables; others also have water and electricity

ASSIGNMENT: First come, first served; and by reservation

REGISTRATION: At camp store

FACILITIES: Hot showers, water spigots, laundry, camp store

PARKING: At campsites only

FEE: $23/night for tent sites, $33/night others

ELEVATION: 7'

RESTRICTIONS:

■ **Pets:** On leash only

■ **Fires:** In fire grates only

■ **Alcohol:** Prohibited

■ **Vehicles:** No van or truck campers permitted in tent area

■ **Other:** 180-day stay limit/year

The other loop has 53 campsites that mostly cater to RVs. During the summer, however, tent campers will use the electrical outlets here to run fans. This loop also has two things that will appeal to tent campers: the bathhouse with hot showers and a covered and screened-in dining area for rainy days or buggy nights. Actually, the mosquitoes aren't as bad as you would imagine, but the swamp angels do come out in summer after heavy rains. In winter, they aren't too bad at all. The campground fills on holiday weekends winter and summer, but other than that, you should be able to get a site. Reservations can be made, and once here you may want to make a reservation to get your preferred site.

The main action is down at the boat ramp. Almost everyone who comes here explores the ultraclear Chassahowitzka River, situated within the protected confines of the 31,000-acre Chassahowitzka National Wildlife Refuge. If you do not have your own watercraft, you can rent canoes, kayaks, johnboats, and even paddleboards. It's a long paddle out to the Gulf, but there are many creeks to be explored in addition to the main waterway. Anglers vie for bream and largemouth bass close to the springhead and salty fish the closer you get to the Gulf. Try to come down in the evening as paddlers and anglers are pulling in. Stores and shopping centers are conveniently located nearby on US 19.

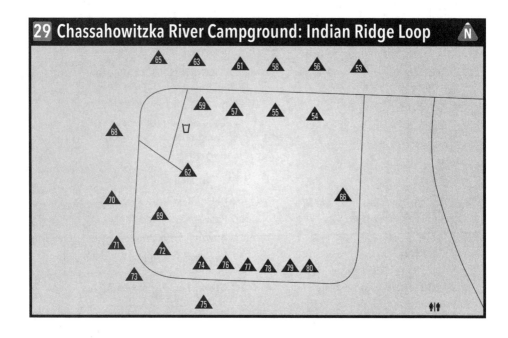

:: Getting There

From Brooksville, take US 98 West 16 miles to intersect US 19 near Chassahowitzka.
From this intersection, take Citrus County Road 480 west 1.7 miles to bear right into
the campground.

GPS COORDINATES   N28° 42′ 51.5″ W82° 34′ 35.3″

30

Clearwater Lake Campground

This lake truly is clear and the campground a clear choice for a rewarding tent camper's outing.

Clearwater Lake Recreation Area is an Ocala National Forest classic—updated to our times, of course. Set on the scenic shores of truly translucent Clearwater Lake, this campground has the right number of sites where you can be assured of getting one of those camps under a shade-bearing live oak, or perhaps even a coveted lakeside site. Not only does the attractive campground complement the fine 32-acre lake, but visitors have an array of outdoor activities right outside the tent door.

But let's start with the campground, staffed by on-site attendants, keeping things safe and orderly. Laid out in two loops, the campground stands on a gently sloping hill extending toward Clearwater

Lake. Overhead, live oaks stretching out their powerful limbs in graceful arcs, along with slash pines and a few palms, shade the camping area. Dense underbrush provides good campsite privacy between the generally large and widespread campsites.

Loop 1, with sites 1–23, seems more popular with tent campers. The first few sites are more open and piney, but then live oaks take over. Campsite 8 is recommended, though it is away from the water. Starting with campsite 13, you come to sites overlooking Clearwater Lake. Campsite 15 is my favorite and where I try to stay every visit, with a good watery view as well as access to the shore and the nature trail circling the tarn. Campsites 16, 18, and 19, each facing toward the water, are large and popular. Luckily, reservations can be made here. The paved loop road then passes the day-use area, with picnic tables, a swim beach, and a kayak/canoe launch. The bathhouse is also located here. Solitude lovers will like campsite 22 or 23, set on their own.

Loop 2 is larger, with 18 very big campsites under live oaks. The sizeable sites

:: Ratings

BEAUTY: ★ ★ ★ ★
PRIVACY: ★ ★ ★ ★
SPACIOUSNESS: ★ ★ ★ ★ ★
QUIET: ★ ★ ★ ★
SECURITY: ★ ★ ★ ★ ★
CLEANLINESS: ★ ★ ★ ★ ★

:: Key Information

ADDRESS: 24511 County Road 42
Paisley, FL 32767

OPERATED BY: American Land &
Leisure, Ocala National Forest

CONTACT: 352-669-0078, www.fs
.usda.gov/ocala; reservations
877-444-6777, recreation.gov

OPEN: Year-round

SITES: 42

EACH SITE: Picnic table, fire ring,
upright grill, lantern post

ASSIGNMENT: First come, first served;
and by reservation

REGISTRATION: At entrance station

FACILITIES: Hot showers, flush toilets,
water spigots

PARKING: At campsites only

FEE: $20/night

ELEVATION: 70'

RESTRICTIONS:

■ **Pets:** On leash only

■ **Fires:** In fire grates only

■ **Alcohol:** At campsite only

■ **Vehicles:** Park only on paved
campsite pads

■ **Other:** Golf carts and electric
scooters prohibited

attract more big rigs. The camps slope down toward Clearwater Lake. Handicapped-accessible sites are located inside the loop. The best site over here is 34. It is closest to the water and offers solitude aplenty.

So what do you do first after setting up camp? A visit to the lake is in order. Water activities are centered on the day-use area, where a swim beach attracts kids and adults alike. A grassy shoreline limits water access from other areas than the swim beach, though a few canoe/kayak launches can be found along the campground shoreline. Anglers will be vying for bream and largemouth bass from shore and also from kayaks, canoes, and small johnboats. Others will be paddling the water for fun, scenery, and exercise. Canoes can be rented here by the hour or by the day.

Walkers can make a loop around the lake on the 1.3-mile Clearwater Lake Nature Trail. Soak in varied views of the water, as well as trips through tall pines and live oak copses, while you stretch your legs. Luckily, the Florida Trail begins its 60-mile journey through the Ocala National Forest at Clearwater Lake. Pick up the Florida Trail and wander through undulating woods as far as your legs will allow, tracing the orange blazes. Or you can take the Paisley Woods Bicycle Trail (also starting here) and roll your way through this section of the Ocala on two interconnected 11-mile bike loops. Ice and wood can be purchased at the camp entrance station. Bring your other supplies, and then you can walk, pedal, and paddle yourself silly; later, return to your fine campsite at Clearwater Lake.

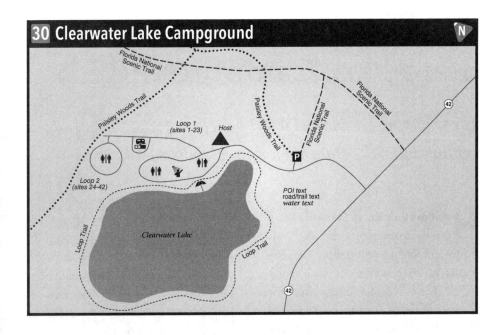

:: Getting There

From the intersection of County Road 42 and FL 19 in Altoona, take CR 42 east toward Paisley 6.4 miles to reach the Clearwater Lake Recreation Area entrance road on your left.

GPS COORDINATES   N28° 58′ 53.4″ W81° 33′ 23.7″

31

Hillsborough River State Park Campground

The US Army established a fort here in the 1830s. Nearly a century later, the state of Florida established a state park.

Hillsborough River State Park has been providing tent campers with a fun and scenic destination for generations. The river here has some actual rapids. This was also a strategic spot for a river crossing during the Seminole Wars; the US Army established a fort here in the 1830s. Nearly a century later, the state of Florida established a state park here for your enjoyment.

The campground is divided into two loops, Hammock and River's Edge. The Hammock Loop has 32 sites. A forest of large live oak and mature pine makes for a dense forest canopy. A thin understory of palmetto divides the mostly open sites. A comfort station with hot showers, flush

:: Ratings

BEAUTY: ★ ★ ★
PRIVACY: ★ ★ ★
SPACIOUSNESS: ★ ★ ★
QUIET: ★ ★ ★
SECURITY: ★ ★ ★ ★ ★
CLEANLINESS: ★ ★ ★ ★

toilets, laundry, and sinks for washing dishes centers the Hammock Loop. The sites close to the comfort station are more open. The River's Edge Loop contains 79 campsites but is really divided into two loops of its own. The right-hand loop has 46 sites beneath a forest, much like the Hammock Loop except with more palm trees. The center of the loop is an open grassy field with a play area for kids. A fully equipped comfort station is on the far side of the loop as you enter. The best sites, and those always in demand, are the seven campsites that back up to the river. River's Edge includes seven wheelchair-accessible sites, 51A–51D and 71–73.

The left-hand loop contains 33 campsites. Pines are more prevalent in this loop, and the palmetto understory is much thicker, allowing better campsite privacy for the campers. The campsites get bigger as you continue along the loop.

A fully equipped comfort station, minus laundry facilities, is in this loop. Campsites are spread along both sides of the road but provide the most privacy

:: Key Information

ADDRESS: Hillsborough River State Park, 15402 US 301 North Thonotosassa, FL 33592

OPERATED BY: Florida State Parks

CONTACT: 813-987-6771, floridastate parks.org; reservations 800-326-3521, reserveamerica.com

OPEN: Year-round

SITES: 112

EACH SITE: Picnic table, fire ring, water spigot, electricity

ASSIGNMENT: Online or assigned by ranger

REGISTRATION: Online, by phone, or at park entrance booth

FACILITIES: Shower, flush toilets, laundry

PARKING: At campsites and extra car parking

FEE: $24/night

ELEVATION: 45'

RESTRICTIONS:

■ **Pets:** On 6-foot leash only

■ **Fires:** In fire rings only

■ **Alcohol:** Prohibited

■ **Vehicles:** None

■ **Other:** 14-day stay limit (seasonally)

in the entire campground. Tent campers will want to stay in this loop.

A series of nature trails follows the river, informing you about the native flora of the region. They leave from the picnic area and connect to the short Rapids Trail. Two bridges span the Hillsborough River and lead to more hiking opportunities. You can cross either the suspension bridge or the stationary bridge to access the Baynard Nature Trail, which explores the hardwood hammock of the river floodplain. The trail was named for a previous superintendent of the park.

The Hillsborough River Hiking Trail makes a 3.3-mile loop across the river. It parallels the watercourse, then veers back northeast, crossing several boardwalks through cypress swamps. Cross the stationary bridge and turn left to begin this trail. The Wetlands Trail makes a round-trip 3-mile hike through an area restored to its natural wetlands environment. It is designed for use by both bikers and hikers. Bicycles, including the two-person Surrey bikes, can be rented at the park.

Paddling the Hillsborough is always fun. Canoes and kayaks can be rented on-site, and you can fish for bass, bream, or catfish. Watch out for those rapids. No swimming is allowed in the river; instead, there is a large swimming pool that is open during warmer months.

On weekends (seasonally), guided tours of Fort Foster are conducted. Self-guided tours are the only way to go during the week. Either way, you will see the

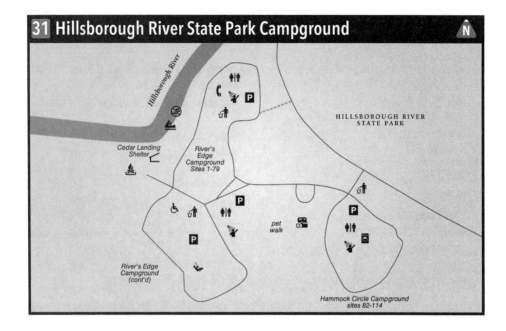

31 Hillsborough River State Park Campground

reconstructed fort and the bridge it pro-tected. You can gain insight into the way of life for a soldier in the 1830s, fighting in the Second Seminole War.

Nowadays, you may have to bat-tle a few campers for space on winter weekends. Snowbirds will plant them-selves down here and make finding a site more challenging during this time,

and spring break can be busy too. Make a reservation to be sure of a site. After the first of April, things slow down. Summer weekdays are quiet, but swim-mers will come here on weekends. Fall can be a good time to float the river. Get your supplies in nearby Zephyrhills and get to camping at Hillsborough River State Park.

:: Getting There

From Zephyrhills, drive south on US 301 for 6 miles. Hillsborough River State Park will be on your right.

GPS COORDINATES   N28° 8′ 42.3″, W82° 13′ 31.5″

32

Hog Island Recreation Area Campground

There are no bad sites in this intimate campground.

Hog Island Campground sits along the dark and alluring Withlacoochee River. Within the confines of the Withlacoochee State Forest, Hog Island enjoys the beauty of the surrounding woodland in addition to the serpentine Withlacoochee River, a designated Florida State Paddling Trail. Though holidays and weekends bring their fair share of visitors, Hog Island retains a quiet and relaxed atmosphere that tent campers enjoy.

The campground is actually across the river from Hog Island. A packed-sand road divides the thick riverside forest, forming a teardrop-shaped loop that circles the campground. Live oak, hickory, and maple trees, draped in Spanish moss, keep the campground shaded. Palmetto and smaller trees form a dense

understory dividing the well-dispersed sites. Squirrels scamper about the campground as if they own it.

There are no sites abutting the Withlacoochee that are open to car campers; however, there is a special riverside campsite reserved for canoe/kayak campers making their way downstream. Southern cypress trees line the river as it encircles Hog Island.

The first few sites at the beginning of the loop are the most open. Campsites are situated along both the inside and outside of the loop. As you near the river, the campsites become more frequented but not worn-down. After passing the riverbank picnic area, the loop passes the bathhouse. The bathhouse is lighted and has electrical outlets near the sinks. Flush toilets and hot showers complete the ensemble.

The best campsites are those on the loop beyond the bathhouse. Sawn logs form campground stools at each site. The sandy campground floor is carpeted with fallen leaves from the hardwood forest. I've never seen sites so widely scattered. Thirsty campers will be relieved to know that each campsite has its own spigot.

:: Ratings

BEAUTY: ★ ★ ★ ★
PRIVACY: ★ ★ ★ ★
SPACIOUSNESS: ★ ★ ★ ★ ★
QUIET: ★ ★ ★
SECURITY: ★ ★
CLEANLINESS: ★ ★ ★

:: Key Information

ADDRESS: Hog Island Recreation Area 15003 Broad St., Brooksville, FL 34601	**ASSIGNMENT:** First come, first served; no reservations
OPERATED BY: Florida Division of Forestry	**REGISTRATION:** Self-registration on-site
CONTACT: 352-797-4140, freshfrom florida.com/Divisions-Offices/Florida-Forest-Service/Our-Forests/State-Forests/Withlacoochee-State-Forest/The-Croom-Tract-at-Withlacoochee-State-Forest	**FACILITIES:** Showers, flush toilets
	PARKING: At campsites only
	FEE: $15/night
	ELEVATION: 90′
OPEN: Year-round	**RESTRICTIONS:**
SITES: 20	■ **Pets:** Prohibited
EACH SITE: Picnic table, fire ring, water spigot	■ **Fires:** In fire rings only
	■ **Alcohol:** Prohibited
	■ **Vehicles:** 1 vehicle/site
	■ **Other:** 14-day stay limit

However, be forewarned that the one bathhouse will be a walk for those on the far side of this sizable loop.

But what is a little walk in this beautiful place? There are two trails directly accessible from the campground. The Hog Island Nature Trail weaves through the riverine woods, making a 1.75-mile loop. I hiked the path in the early morning hours, spotting three deer, while following the numbered posts explaining the various components of the Withlacoochee basin ecosystems.

Hog Island is part of the Tract of the Withlacoochee State Forest. Just before the campground loop, a trail runs roughly parallel to the river south for 6.8 miles to Silver Lake. Silver Lake is basically a wide spot in the Withlacoochee, just below the confluence of the Withlacoochee and Little Withlacoochee Rivers.

In addition to these trails, there are 25 more miles of hiking to enjoy in the tract. These trails meander through a host of environments, from live oak thickets, to pine stands, to open prairie lands, as well as through signs of human habitation, old homesites, and abandoned mines.

If you want to enjoy the Withlacoochee River, take a canoe or kayak. There is a boat launch right next to the campground. There are two more launches upstream at Iron Bridge and Silver Lake. If you are boatless, several outfitters in nearby Nobleton, just downstream on County Road 476, will be happy to rent you a boat. Convenient but costly supplies can be purchased here

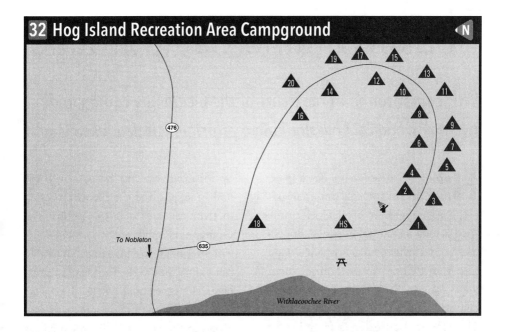

too. A quiet float downriver is an ideal way to observe wildlife. I've paddled the entire Withlacoochee from beginning to end—the scenery is guaranteed.

There are no bad sites in this intimate campground. But don't expect everything to be perfect here; it's managed by the Florida Division of Forestry. They do the best they can with available resources. And with the lush woodland and scenic river, they had fine natural resources with which to start.

:: Getting There

From Nobleton, drive east on CR 476. Then turn right on CR 635 and drive 1 mile to a 4-way intersection. Continue forward on the dirt road 300 yards; Hog Island Campground will be on your right.

GPS COORDINATES   N28° 36' 57.4" W82° 14' 19.7"

33

Hopkins Prairie Campground

This campground in the heart of the Ocala has camps under live-oak woodland overlooking a prairie-encircled lake.

Hopkins Prairie is a regular stop on my visits to the Ocala National Forest. The campground itself, albeit primitive, is long on natural beauty. A finger-like strand of live oaks stretches deep into a grassy and watery prairie where views can be had from nearly every campsite. It is also strategically located. The Florida Trail extends for miles in both directions, and the open-water portions of the prairie allow watery recreation. Finally, a nearby water-filled sink offers swimming possibilities.

The 21-site campground is spread over a large area. Most sites have good privacy, though a few are open to one another. The campground rarely fills, making privacy even more viable. A campground host mans the entrance. Each site is shaded

:: Ratings

BEAUTY: ★ ★ ★ ★ ★
PRIVACY: ★ ★ ★
SPACIOUSNESS: ★ ★ ★ ★ ★
QUIET: ★ ★ ★ ★ ★
SECURITY: ★ ★ ★
CLEANLINESS: ★ ★ ★ ★

by artistically curving live oaks with the limbs merging and their leaves meeting to form canopies over the camps. The campground splits and the main loop, with sites 11–18, extends a finger of shaded camps into the prairie. The views are great here. The other road houses three sites that overlook the prairie and have easy access to the Florida Trail, which comes in near site 21. A bat house stands here to help curb the mosquitoes.

From site 21, the northbound portion of the Florida Trail skirts Hopkins Prairie, the largest prairie in the Ocala, offering numerous vistas for the hiker. It then leaves the large wetland for a region of smaller prairies to enter longleaf–wire grass woodland, once prevalent over Florida. This rolling land of towering pines and knee-high, swaying wire grass offers vistas of its own. This section of the Florida Trail deserves more recognition for its beauty. Southbound on the Florida Trail, hikers will cross the campground entrance road, then reach a watery sink after 0.9 mile. Steps lead into the water, and it is a great place to take a dip. It is 2.3 miles farther to reach the Yearling Trail. Here, a spur trail leads

:: Key Information

ADDRESS: Ocala National Forest, Lake George Ranger District, 17147 E FL 40, Silver Springs, FL 34488

OPERATED BY: US Forest Service

CONTACT: 352-625-2520, www.fs.usda.gov/ocala

OPEN: October–May

SITES: 21

EACH SITE: Picnic table, fire ring, lantern post; some have upright grill

ASSIGNMENT: First come, first served; no reservations

REGISTRATION: Self-registration

FACILITIES: Crank well, vault toilet

PARKING: At campsites only

FEE: $10/night

ELEVATION: 45′

RESTRICTIONS:

■ **Pets:** On leash only

■ **Fires:** In fire grates only

■ **Alcohol:** At campsites only

■ **Vehicles:** None

■ **Other:** 14-day stay limit

left 0.6 mile to Pats Island and the Long Cemetery. The book *The Yearling* was made into a movie starring Gregory Peck and was filmed on-site. Marjorie Kinnan Rawlings, the author of *The Yearling*, stayed with the last two residents of Pats Island, Calvin and Mary Long, which gave her book great authenticity, capturing the lives of these early Florida pioneers. Pats Island was abandoned for good in 1935. From the cemetery, turn left on the spur trail and head 0.3 mile to a large, dry sinkhole. This cemetery and nearby sinkhole can also be accessed via the Yearling Trailhead on FL 19. Watery pursuits include canoeing or kayaking on Hopkins Prairie. The lake is picturesque, its waters rimmed in tawny grasses. A hand boat launch is near campsite 18. Anglers can vie for bream or largemouth bass. You can also visit Silver Glen Springs, a great swimming destination, accessible from FL 19 south of Hopkins Prairie.

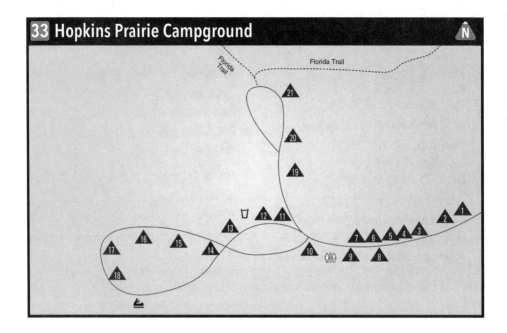

:: Getting There

From Ocala, head east on FL 40 for 12 miles to Marion County Road 314. Turn left on CR 314 and follow it 18 miles to FL 19. Turn right on FL 19 and follow it 7.8 miles to Forest Route 50. Turn right on FR 50 and follow it 2.4 miles to FR 50F. Turn right on FR 50F and follow it 0.7 mile to the campground.

GPS COORDINATES   N29° 16' 35.4" W81° 41' 34.4"

34

Juniper Springs Recreation Area Campground

The springs stay 72°F year-round, and the warm days
and cool nights make for ideal camping conditions.

This recreation area was developed well in the 1930s and is well taken care of today. Clear, 72°F Juniper Springs is the centerpiece of this Ocala National Forest landmark. The springs well up at 13 million gallons per day into continental America's only subtropical national forest. The campground is aesthetically integrated into the landscape and has a separate loop for tent campers only.

The campground is divided into three loops. The first loop is the 34-site Tropic Camp Area. Palm trees, live oak, and southern hardwoods shade the campsites, which have adequate privacy thanks to the understory of palmetto. The 17 campsites on the outside of the paved loop are pull-through sites designed for RVs. The

:: Ratings

BEAUTY: ★ ★ ★ ★ ★
PRIVACY: ★ ★ ★
SPACIOUSNESS: ★ ★ ★
QUIET: ★ ★ ★
SECURITY: ★ ★ ★ ★ ★
CLEANLINESS: ★ ★ ★ ★

pull-in sites on the inside of the loop have less room but are closer to one of the two modern comfort stations. Warm showers are available in one of the comfort stations. Though this loop is attractive, the presence of RVs makes it the least appealing loop.

The Sandpine Camp Area has 25 drive-up campsites on a paved loop. A primarily pine canopy makes for a brighter, more open campsite. Thick vegetation buffers yield the maximum in privacy. The eight campsites on the inside of the loop are closer to the centrally located comfort station and its flush toilets for each sex. However, there is no shower. This is the second-most-desirable and least used loop.

The best loop is the Fern Hammock Tent Camp Area. The paved road ends, and the campsites begin beneath a tall canopy of palm trees and southern hardwoods such as hickory. Three campsites on the main road are immediately followed by a spur loop with seven sites near a low-lying area.

Four campsites are on a small dead end beside Fern Hammock Springs. The other five campsites are near the loop

:: Key Information

ADDRESS: Juniper Springs Recreation Area, 26701 FL 40 Silver Springs, FL 34488

OPERATED BY: US Forest Service and Recreation Resources Management

CONTACT: 352-625-3147, www.fs .usda.gov/ocala; reservations 877-444-6777, recreation.gov

OPEN: Year-round

SITES: 79

EACH SITE: Tent pad, concrete picnic table, fire ring, lantern post

ASSIGNMENT: First come, first served; and by reservation

REGISTRATION: Online, by phone, and at campground entrance booth

FACILITIES: Showers, flush toilets, water spigots , camp store, canoe rentals

PARKING: At campsites only

FEE: $21/night

ELEVATION: 45'

RESTRICTIONS:

■ **Pets:** On leash only

■ **Fires:** In fire rings only

■ **Alcohol:** At campsites only

■ **Vehicles:** None

■ **Other:** March–September, 14-day stay limit; October–February, 30-day stay limit

comfort station, which has warm showers. This loop has the thinnest understory, mostly ground cover; however, this will give you a chance to meet your fellow tent campers.

Water spigots are well placed throughout this attractive, carefully maintained campground. Overall, the campsites are spacious, clean, and camper friendly.

Summer weekends are the busy time here; the campground will fill. But other than that, you should have no problem getting a campsite. Winter is a good time to visit; mosquitoes are less of a problem. The springs stay at 72°F year-round, and the warm days and cool nights make for ideal camping conditions.

Juniper Springs attracts swimmers no matter what the season. The Civilian Conservation Corps lined the area where the water bubbles up with concrete and rock. The springs serve as a natural swimming pool. Concrete steps lead into the waters, where snorkelers kick around amid sunbathers cooling off from the Florida sun.

Trails lead through all of the camping loops to both Fern Hammock and Juniper springs. A 0.75-mile-long, self-interpretive nature trail starts at Juniper Springs and follows Juniper Creek. Learn about this ecosystem that features flora and fauna of north and south Florida.

The most popular activity here at Juniper Springs is paddling. A 7-mile, one-way trip leads from the springs to Juniper Wayside Park near Lake George. Float the translucent waters on the narrow creek

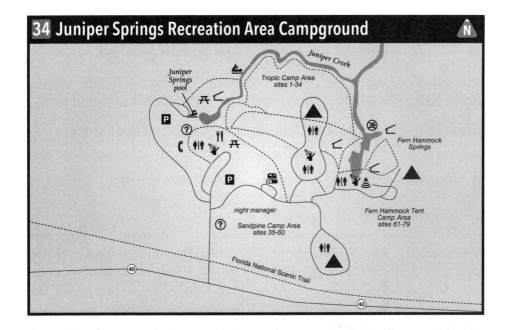

through the heart of the 13,000-acre Juniper Prairie Wilderness. Cypress trees line the waterway, along with palms and other hardwoods. Motorboat enthusiasts have nearby Lake George, Florida's second-largest lake, in which to enjoy all manner of water activities.

Long- or short-distance hikers can enjoy a portion of the Florida National Scenic Trail. It heads in either direction near the campground entrance booth. The northerly portion of the trail enters the Juniper Prairie Wilderness, passing many small lakes and Juniper Creek itself before leaving the wilderness after 9 miles.

Come and enjoy this natural, well-cared-for showpiece of the Ocala National Forest.

:: Getting There

From Ocala, drive east on FL 40 for 28 miles. Juniper Springs Recreation Area will be on your left.

GPS COORDINATES   N29° 10' 58.9" W81° 42' 42.9"

Lake Eaton Campground

Lake Eaton has fine fishing, and the pier is a good place to watch the clouds roll by. Relaxation comes naturally here.

Lake Eaton Campground is located on the shores of Lake Eaton, amidst a forest of tall pines and live oaks, which spread their shade-giving branches throughout the area. A scattering of sabal palms graces the forest, affording it that semitropical look. A thick ground cover of brushy oaks and a smattering of palmettos lend an in-the-forest feel to this campground.

The camping area is organized in the classic loop fashion, stretched out along a packed-dirt road. The first three campsites are single sites on the outside of the loop. Campsite 1, at the beginning of the loop, is somewhat open, but after that, the woods take over. These sites are very spacious, but the double sites, 4–6, are large. They are set back farther on the loop and have two concrete picnic tables

:: Ratings

BEAUTY: ★ ★ ★ ★
PRIVACY: ★ ★ ★ ★
SPACIOUSNESS: ★ ★ ★ ★ ★
QUIET: ★ ★ ★ ★ ★
SECURITY: ★ ★ ★
CLEANLINESS: ★ ★ ★

each. The pine needles and oak leaves get rather thick back here.

The next five campsites are on the outside of the loop as it doubles back around. These sites are the most private. However, nearly all the campsites at Lake Eaton feature superlative privacy and spaciousness. These five sites are closest to Lake Eaton and have a somewhat obscured view of the water. The final three campsites are large single sites and are the only sites on the inside of the campground loop.

A pit toilet for each sex lies in the center of the loop. No water is available— bring your own. These rustic facilities encourage hardier tent campers, though a few RV-driving snowbirds can be seen here during the winter. Tent campers are the norm year-round. Don't imagine some rough place, though. National forest campgrounds are generally less developed.

This locale of natural beauty just needed a little organization, and it got it. The Forest Service has built a boat ramp, but this body of water spells paddling for me. A fishing and observation pier has been erected near the campground. Lake Eaton has fine fishing, and the pier

:: Key Information

ADDRESS: Ocala National Forest, Lake George Ranger District, 17147 E FL 40, Silver Springs, FL 34488

OPERATED BY: US Forest Service

CONTACT: 352-625-2520, www.fs.usda.gov/ocala

OPEN: Year-round

SITES: 14

EACH SITE: Picnic table, fire ring, lantern post

ASSIGNMENT: First come, first served; no reservations

REGISTRATION: Self-registration on-site

FACILITIES: Pit toilet

PARKING: At campsites only

FEE: $8/night

ELEVATION: 40′

RESTRICTIONS:

- **Pets:** On 6-foot leash maximum
- **Fires:** In fire rings only
- **Alcohol:** At campsites only
- **Vehicles:** None
- **Other:** 14-day stay limit

is a good place to watch the clouds roll by. Relaxation comes naturally here.

But don't get lazy. There is a pair of trails nearby that would be a shame to miss. Head back out to Forest Route 96, and take a left. Drive about half a mile, then take another left on FR 79. Soon you'll come to the Eaton Sinkhole Trail and the Lake Eaton Loop Trail.

The Sinkhole Trail was the highlight of my day. It forms a 2-mile loop and passes through a sand-scrub forest to a place where the limestone strata, 120 feet below the surface, has eroded. The land above it collapsed and formed the sinkhole, which is approximately 110 feet deep. It resembles an inverted island of moist flora, surrounded by the drier sand-scrub forest. Plaques and displays explain this process. Do not miss this trail.

The 2.1-mile Lake Eaton Loop Trail starts across the road and descends from the dry, hilly woods to the cypress that borders Lake Eaton. Side paths lead to observation points on the lake. When I was there, I tagged along on a guided hike for bird-watchers, then learned I have a long way to go in identifying Florida's varied avian creatures.

Many other nearby natural lakes grace the immediate area. Lake Lou and Fore Lake are two that have forest access. The Ocklawaha River is minutes away and offers a paddling experience of its own. A map of the Ocala National Forest will help you navigate your way through the 430,000 acres it encompasses. No matter what you do in the Ocala National Forest, Lake Eaton will be a fine place to return, as others do, year after year.

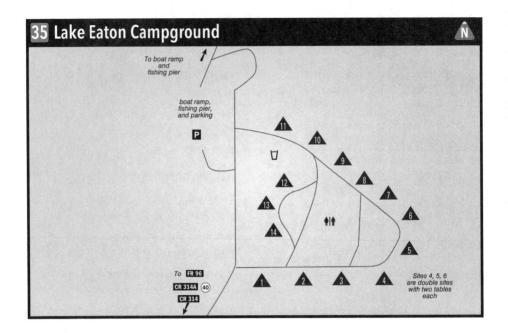

:: Getting There

From Ocala, drive east on FL 40 for about 17 miles. Turn left on CR 314A, follow it about 5 miles, then turn right on FR 96. Follow FR 96 for 0.5 mile. Turn left on FR 96A and drive 1 mile. Lake Eaton Campground will be on your right.

GPS COORDINATES   N29° 15' 14.5" W81° 51' 56.6"

36

Lithia Springs Park Campground

This oak-shaded campground features watery recreation in both springs and rivers.

This **Hillsborough County** park has a lot of natural beauty with which to work. Begin with an attractive piece of terra firma in a gorgeous oak forest situated along a brooding river, then add a crystalline spring emitting 24 million gallons a day, and you have Lithia Springs Park. Now, drop in a campground with just the right number of sites, then stretch the sites well apart underneath the oaks and along the river. Spread crushed shells at each site; then put in water, electricity, a picnic table, and a fire ring for every camp. Add an infrastructure including two nice bathhouses, sprinkle in a few trails, a playground, a picnic area, a designated swimming area, and a canoe

:: Ratings

BEAUTY: ★ ★ ★ ★ ★
PRIVACY: ★ ★ ★ ★
SPACIOUSNESS: ★ ★ ★ ★
QUIET: ★ ★ ★
SECURITY: ★ ★ ★ ★ ★
CLEANLINESS: ★ ★ ★ ★

launch. Finally, throw in some helpful park personnel, and you have this fine destination conveniently located in the greater Tampa Bay area.

The campground is spaced out along a paved loop road with numerous speed bumps. Nothing special about that. It is the sites and the setting in which they lie that makes this a desirable destination. You will immediately notice that the sites are large or average-size at worst. Younger live oaks reach high for the sky, growing together on their upper sides to canopy the campsites, leaving them well shaded. A thick buffer of younger oaks, palmetto, and other brush grows between the campsites to provide good campsite privacy. Additionally, many of the campsites are set deeply back from the campground loop road, lending more privacy. Spanish moss grows on anything that doesn't move. Ferns thrive in the shade. Cedars and pines also shade the camps. The second camping cluster has the advantage of sites along the Alafia River. These four sites—33, 35, 37, and 38—are the first to be snapped up.

:: Key Information

ADDRESS: 3932 Lithia Springs Road Lithia, FL 33547	**REGISTRATION:** At campground office
OPERATED BY: Hillsborough County Parks	**FACILITIES:** Hot showers, flush toilets
	PARKING: At campsites only
CONTACT: 813-744-5572, hillsboroughcounty.org	**FEE:** $24/night
	ELEVATION: 22′
OPEN: Year-round	**RESTRICTIONS:**
SITES: 40	■ **Pets:** On leash only
EACH SITE: Picnic table, fire ring, water, electricity	■ **Fires:** In fire grates only
	■ **Alcohol:** Prohibited
ASSIGNMENT: First come, first served; no reservations	■ **Vehicles:** 2 vehicles/site
	■ **Other:** 14-day stay limit

Two bathhouses are conveniently placed for access to the two main camping clusters. The campground host makes things easier, as do park personnel. The ratio of RVs to tent campers is about 50:50. Unfortunately, they are not separated. However, tent campers need not worry, as the setup seems to work for all. Be apprised that no reservations are accepted, so you take your chances. The campground fills on holiday weekends year-round and on cool-weather winter weekends.

Campers and noncampers alike flock to the springs for which the park is named. A circular pool, centered by a vent and surrounded by sand, attracts young and old swimmers alike. Paddlers like to float the Alafia River. A canoe launch makes trips easy. Paddlers can make the 10-mile run from Alderman's Ford Park to Lithia

Springs. This section of the Alafia meanders through beautiful oak and cypress woodlands. The banks are occasionally 8–10 feet high. In most places, though, the shoreline is shallow and sandy. There is a little private property along the river, so be sure to respect the property rights of others. But most of the land is county preserve. Between Alderman's Ford and Lithia Springs, there are at least six sets of mild whitewater rapids. Also, you can make the 7.5-mile paddle from Lithia Springs to the Alafia boat ramp off Alafia Boulevard. The first 3 miles of this section contain some of the most scenic landscapes on the entire Alafia. Huge oaks line high banks, and the tree canopy shades up to 75% of the river area. Four miles downstream of the put-in, the Alafia passes beneath Bell Shoals Bridge (no

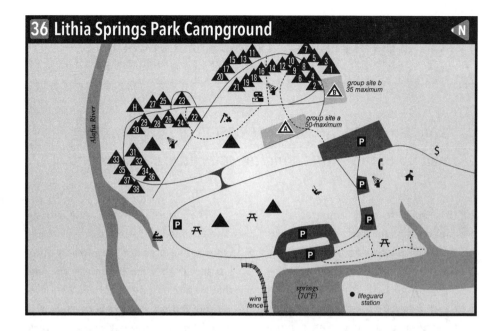

access), and from this point on the shoreline becomes highly developed. The river broadens and becomes quite sluggish. For the next 3.5 miles to the take-out, the paddler will likely encounter powerboat traffic. Whether you opt for the river or the springs, your base camp at Lithia Springs Park will be a winner.

:: Getting There

To reach the campground from Exit 254 on I-75, take US 301 South to Bloomingdale Avenue. Turn left and head east on Bloomingdale Avenue. Follow Bloomingdale Avenue to Lithia-Pinecrest Road/County Road 640. Turn right and head southeast on Lithia-Pinecrest Road, and follow it beyond the bridge over the Alafia River. Just ahead, turn right on Lithia Springs Road to reach Lithia Springs Park.

GPS COORDINATES   N27° 51′ 58.9″ W82° 13′ 47.8″

37

Mutual Mine Recreation Area Campground

Time, nature, and the Florida Division of Forestry have teamed up to make this a picturesque little campground.

This state-forest campground is underutilized. Some folks are put off because it's located around an abandoned phosphate mine. Don't worry—it's safe around here. The lake filled in with rainwater after the hand-dug mine was abandoned in 1914. That's more than 100 years ago! Eventually, time, nature, and the Florida Division of Forestry have teamed up to make this a picturesque little campground. The forestry people have also constructed many miles of hiking trails nearby, and Mutual Mine is now home to fish only. Florida's most unusual state park, Homosassa Springs State Wildlife Park, is just a short drive away.

:: Ratings

BEAUTY: ★ ★ ★ ★ ★
PRIVACY: ★ ★ ★
SPACIOUSNESS: ★ ★ ★ ★ ★
QUIET: ★ ★
SECURITY: ★ ★ ★
CLEANLINESS: ★ ★ ★ ★

The Mutual Mine Campground entrance road splits into two spur roads. One road has six campsites, and the other has seven. They are divided by the lake that was once Mutual Mine. The level ground above the mine is covered by a mixed forest of live oak and pine trees. The campground has a grassy understory that seems like a lawn.

The spur road to the right enters an open forest of mature pines. It seems as if the area has been landscaped. The first two campsites are in this pinewoods, which is carpeted by needles over the grass. The campsites are open and spacious. The next two campsites are shaded by live oaks and a stray turkey oak.

There is a large space between all the campsites, which makes up for the lack of understory. The spur road ends in a loop and holds the final two sites, which are in a thicket of laurel and live oak. These sites are spacious as well and have an obscured view of the lake.

The western spur road also begins in an open pine forest. The first campsite is obscured by young trees, but

:: Key Information

ADDRESS: Mutual Mine Recreation Area, 15003 Broad St. Brooksville, FL 34601

OPERATED BY: Florida Division of Forestry

CONTACT: 352-797-4140, freshfromflorida.com/Divisions-Offices/Florida-Forest-Service/Our-Forests/State-Forests/Withlacoochee-State-Forest/Recreation-at-Withlacoochee-State-Forest

OPEN: Daily Labor Day–Memorial Day; weekends only during summer months

SITES: 13

EACH SITE: Picnic table, fire ring with grill

ASSIGNMENT: First come, first served; no reservations

REGISTRATION: Ranger will come by and register you

FACILITIES: Flush toilets, water spigots

PARKING: At campsites only

FEE: $15/night

ELEVATION: 50'

RESTRICTIONS:

- **Pets:** Prohibited
- **Fires:** In fire ring or grill only
- **Alcohol:** Prohibited
- **Vehicles:** 1 vehicle/site

the next four are in the pines and have immense "yards" on which to stake a tent. Live oaks begin at the fourth site. Wooden poles divide the sites on this loop road as well.

The road bends around the lake and includes two very private sites, where the woods are dense and the shade is heavy. The two sites are separated from each other and the rest of the campground by trees and distance. Farther along, the spur road turns around.

This attractive campground feels small already, but the two spur roads make it look like two distinct campgrounds. The two roads share a common restroom area, located at the beginning of the right-hand road. There are two

shedlike structures that house clean flush toilets for each sex. Water spigots are located throughout the campground.

You can get a closer look into the old mine via the nature trail that winds along the lake's shoreline. It starts at the wooden stairway leading down to it. The half-hour walk goes up and down along the steep banks of the lake. Though the lake may be partly covered in algae, a ranger told me the fishing was good here. The lake can be accessed at several points along the rugged little trail.

Also at the campground is a trailhead for the 46 miles of trails in the Citrus Tract of the Withlacoochee State Forest. A board at the trailhead shows you the loop possibilities. Maps are available online as

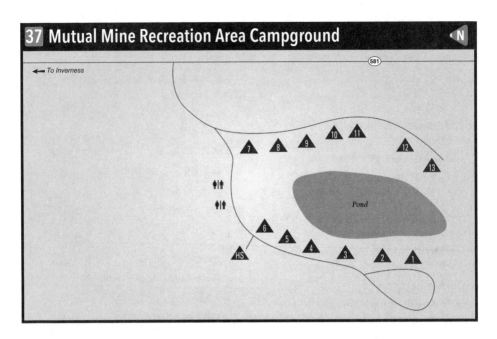

well. The Citrus Hiking Trail is blazed in orange. You can stay dry-footed (providing it doesn't rain, which happened during my trip here) and pass through several forest communities, including sandhill scrub, stands of turkey oak, and live oak thickets. The hiking combinations are limited only by your stamina, though Mansfield Pond is a good destination.

At Homosassa Springs Wildlife Park you can see all sorts of wild animals, including bears, bobcats, and birds. Boat tours of the Springs of 10,000 Fish are available. You will probably see a manatee. Because the park is state run, you know this is not some fly-by-night sideshow. Check it out. It is west of Inverness on US 19.

Mutual Mine is an off-the-beaten-path campground where RVs are as rare as the bad experiences. Pick your site in the pines or beneath the live oaks. Just remember to make sure it is on a Friday, Saturday, or Sunday night if you go during the months of June, July, or August.

:: Getting There

From US 41 in Inverness, drive west 0.5 mile on FL 44. Turn left on County Road 581 and follow it 5 miles. Mutual Mine will be on your right.

GPS COORDINATES   N28° 43′ 14.7″ W82° 19′ 1.2″

38

Starkey Wilderness Park Campground

This Pasco County Park is part of a 12,000-acre water-management preserve that has trails aplenty.

Back in the 1930s, Mr. Jay B. Starkey began a cattle operation in what was then rural Pasco County. Later, he worked out a deal with Southwest Florida Water Management District; his land, encompassing parts of the Anclote and Pithlachasotee Rivers, is now a large wilderness area and well field for coastal Pasco County. It's topped off with a first-rate campground designed for tent campers only. Outdoor enthusiasts can use the campground as a jumping-off point to explore foot trails, equestrian paths, and a special 7-mile paved trail that is popular with hikers and bikers alike. Be apprised that the campground is nice enough that you may not want to "jump off" from it, but instead just relax in your wooded civilization-escape zone.

Enter the campground loop. Ample oaks and pines provide shade. Palmetto islands form barriers between many of the sites. The camps are generally large and spaced far apart from one another. Parking areas are situated along the loop, but all campsites require a short stroll and should be considered walk-in tent sites. Wooden posts keep cars and campers separated. A large picnic shelter is situated across from campsites 1 and 2 and can provide refuge from the elements. As you curve around the campground, sparsely situated sand pines begin to dominate. However, the last part of the loop is actually shaded by live oaks, so you really have your options of whether you want sun or shade. Eight water spigots are scattered along the loop, availing aqua to all campers. A nice, clean bathhouse is located across from campsite 13.

The campground is busiest during winter holidays. Firewood is provided at the campground, but you must retrieve it yourself and tote it to your campsite.

:: Ratings

BEAUTY: ★ ★ ★ ★
PRIVACY: ★ ★ ★ ★
SPACIOUSNESS: ★ ★ ★ ★ ★
QUIET: ★ ★ ★
SECURITY: ★ ★ ★ ★
CLEANLINESS: ★ ★ ★ ★

:: Key Information

ADDRESS: Starkey Wilderness Park
10500 Wilderness Park Blvd.
New Port Richey, FL 34655

OPERATED BY: Pasco County and
Southwest Florida Water Management
District

CONTACT: 727-834-3247,
pascocountyfl.net

OPEN: Year-round

SITES: 16

EACH SITE: Picnic table, fire pit,
upright grill

ASSIGNMENT: First come, first served;
and by reservation

REGISTRATION: At park office

FACILITIES: Hot showers, flush toilets,
water spigots

PARKING: At designated parking
areas only

FEE: $10/night April–September and
$15/night October–March

ELEVATION: 35'

RESTRICTIONS:

■ **Pets:** Prohibited

■ **Fires:** In fire grates only

■ **Alcohol:** Prohibited

■ **Vehicles:** RVs prohibited

■ **Other:** 14-day state limit

Most of the campers here are local and like to hang around the campsite. They will also enjoy the day-use area, located along the banks of the Pithlachasotee River. It offers a play area and a 1.6-mile nature trail. Anglers have fishing opportunities in the river. The park has an additional 25 miles of hiking trails and even provides backpack camping opportunities. The aforementioned 7-mile paved multiuse trail connects to the 42-mile paved Suncoast Trail, allowing bikers to pedal themselves to exhaustion. Get a trail map, and you can make the most of the 12,000-plus-acre preserve no matter your mode of exploration. You may find yourself enjoying both the campground and the outdoor activities.

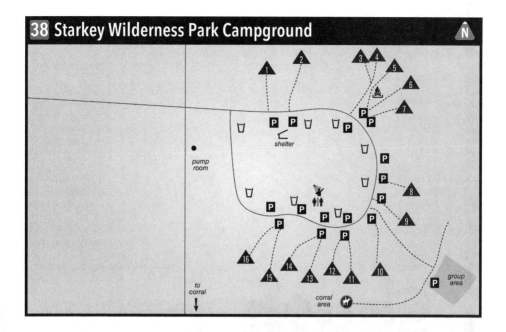

:: Getting There

From Exit 14 on the Suncoast Parkway, take FL 54 West 7.1 miles to Starkey Boulevard. Look for a sign for a development known as Longleaf. Turn right here, on Starkey Boulevard, and follow it 4.5 miles to reach Wilderness Road. Turn right on Wilderness Road and follow it to enter the park.

GPS COORDINATES   N28° 14′ 56″ W82° 36′ 48″

South Florida

39

Bahia Honda State Park Campground

The ecosystem here is as unique as its geographical distinction.

Bahia Honda is Florida's southern-most state park, and therefore the southernmost state park in the United States. And the ecosystem here is as unique as its geographical distinction. Two of the three separate campgrounds here are ideal for tent campers. And the other one, well, that's for the RV gang.

Being so far south and so close to Key West makes Bahia Honda busy, especially in winter. Make your reservations up to 11 months in advance, because only 10% of the sites are first come, first served. Campers tend to plant themselves once they get a site at Bahia Honda. If you must take a site in the RV area, take it, then get on the waiting list to transfer to another site.

The Buttonwood Camping Area is the one for RVs. It is the most open and the closest to US 1. If you have a boat, it has a campside marina just for campers. Buttonwood also has a full bathhouse. Fifteen sites are oceanside, but it seems more like a parking lot by the sea.

The Sandspur Camping Area is closest to Sandspur Beach, consistently rated as one of the best beaches in America. The camping area is not too bad either. It contains 24 campsites arranged in linear fashion along a spur road. The first eight sites are cut into the beachside woodland. The beach is across the spur road. These sites are well shaded but could be hot and buggy on windless days.

Past the bathhouse, campsites are situated on both sides of the road. Five more sites are nestled in the woods.

The other side of the road contains 11 beachside campsites that are the most desirable at Bahia Honda. These campsites, like all those in the Sandspur area, have well-grown campsite buffers.

The Bay Side Camping Area is the smallest and most isolated. You must pass through the Buttonwood Camping Area and drive under the low clearance of US 1, which effectively cuts off all but standard passenger cars and trucks. Pass

:: Ratings

BEAUTY: ★★★★
PRIVACY: ★★★
SPACIOUSNESS: ★★★
QUIET: ★★
SECURITY: ★★★
CLEANLINESS: ★★★

:: Key Information

ADDRESS: Bahia Honda State Park
36850 Overseas Highway
Big Pine Key, FL 33043

OPERATED BY: Florida State Parks

CONTACT: 305-872-2353, floridastate
parks.org; reservations 800-326-3521,
reserveamerica.com

OPEN: Year-round

SITES: 60 electric, 20 nonelectric

EACH SITE: Picnic table, fire grill, water

ASSIGNMENT: Online or assigned by
ranger

REGISTRATION: At park entrance
booth

FACILITIES: Showers, flush toilets

PARKING: At campsites only

FEE: $36/night

ELEVATION: Sea level

RESTRICTIONS:
- **Pets:** On 6-foot leash only
- **Fires:** In fire grills only
- **Alcohol:** Prohibited
- **Vehicles:** 2/site
- **Other:** 14-day stay limit

a restroom and come to the eight wooded sites. These sites, across the road from the Gulf, curve around a small bay.

I recommend the Sandspur Camping Area over the others. It is most suitable for tent campers and is closest to the best beach at Bahia Honda, Sandspur Beach. There are two other beaches here, Calusa Beach and Logger Head Beach. Calusa Beach is in the Gulf but looks out on busy US 1 and is adjacent to the main marina. Logger Head Beach is on the Atlantic and has nothing but a view of those colorful Key waters.

These beaches can get hot any time of year, but each one has swimmer-friendly waters and the best swimming in the Keys. The water is never too cold, even in winter. Anglers enjoy these waters as well. Tarpon, when in season, is the most desired catch. Launch your boat at the marina or hire a guide.

One unusual aspect of Bahia Honda is the old bridge. It is the now-closed span that used to connect Bahia Honda Key with West Summerland Key. A trail to the old bridge leaves near Logger Head Beach. Follow the span as it rises over the waters below. It's probably as high as you will get in the Keys. Another walk is the nature trail that enters the real Florida at the north end of the Sandspur Beach.

No trip this far south is complete without a trip to Key West. Ernest Hemingway's town has its share of over-the-top tourist attractions yet is also layered with history. The narrow roads can be congested, but relax and join in the parade. Check out Duval Street, a mecca for tourists; Old Town's elegant homes; and Mallory Square with its street entertainers.

The best way to do this may seem corny at first, but swallow your pride, don your shades, and ride the Conch Tour

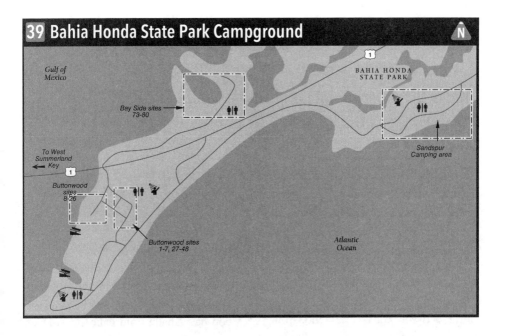

Train. It's the ultimate in tourist schlock, but you will learn much about the history of this southernmost city in the United States. Then you can drive back to your campsite at Bahia Honda with a complete taste of the Keys.

:: Getting There

From Marathon, drive 12 miles south to Bahia Honda Recreation Area. Turn left into the state park entrance.

GPS COORDINATES   N24° 39′ 46.3″ W81° 15′ 48.5

40

Bear Island Campground

*This is the most remote and rustic campground
you will find in this guidebook.*

This is the most secluded and rustic campground you will find in this guidebook. But that is only fitting, for the 729,000-acre Big Cypress National Preserve is a remote and rugged place. Vast tracts of cypress trees, pinewoods, hardwood forests, and grassy prairies intermingle in reaction to the timeless battle between water and land. Your adventure in the Big Cypress is limited only to how daring you are. A system of marked trails emanates from Bear Island Campground, offering a glimpse into a strange and beautiful ecosystem.

Formerly a free—and freewheeling—place, the Big Cypress Preserve has "tamed" Bear Island, putting in designated campsites each with picnic table, fire ring, and lantern post. Many have an elevated tent pad. The campground

begins shortly after the final right turn from Turner River Road, a 20-mile gravel track. After you pass the first old cattle guard, a loop road turns left. This road leads to an open field, bordered on one side by woodland and on the other side by freshwater prairie. Sites 1–12 are scattered here, the sites on the east side of the loop have shade from palm trees, Dade County pine, and a few live oaks.

The main campground continues on the primary road. Here you will see sites situated along either side of the road. Every possible combination of sun, shade, openness, and privacy are available amid palms, pines, and live oaks rising above a grassy floor. There is ample space between most sites. Thick stands of palmetto add privacy.

Some sites are far back from the road and are ringed in palms with pines over them. Other sites back against an open prairie that looks out on stands of cypress in the distance. As you press on, another cattle guard crosses the road. This is the end of the campground and the beginning of a jeep trail system. By the way, get a trail map of the Bear Island area online, at the Big Cypress Visitor Center, or at

:: Ratings

BEAUTY: ★ ★ ★
PRIVACY: ★ ★ ★
SPACIOUSNESS: ★ ★ ★ ★ ★
QUIET: ★ ★ ★
SECURITY: ★ ★
CLEANLINESS: ★ ★

:: Key Information

ADDRESS: Bear Island Campground
52105 Tamiami Trail E
Ochopee, FL 34141

OPERATED BY: Big Cypress National
Preserve

CONTACT: 239-695-1205, nps.gov
/bicy; reservations 800-326-3521,
reserveamerica.com

OPEN: Campsites 1–12 are open
year-round, sites 14–40 are open
August 15–April 15

SITES: 39

EACH SITE: Picnic table, fire ring,
lantern post

ASSIGNMENT: First come, first served;
and by reservation

REGISTRATION: Online

FACILITIES: Vault toilets, bring your
own water

PARKING: At campsites only

FEE: $10

ELEVATION: 15'

RESTRICTIONS:

■ **Pets:** On 6-foot leash maximum
■ **Fires:** In fire rings only
■ **Alcohol:** At campsites only
■ **Vehicles:** None

the Wildlife Check-In Station near the campground.

Bear Island often is used by tenters who like their sites distant and primitive, hunters, off-road vehicle enthusiasts, and some snowbirds. This place is very remote, but its remoteness is two sided. Because most people won't casually venture here, your privacy is virtually guaranteed. The downside, however, is that help, should you require it, could be a long time in coming. I popped a tire here one time and had a long, slow drive to Naples on a temporary spare for repair. Still, I wouldn't worry about it beyond taking normal precautions. I firmly believe you are safer in nearly any wilderness setting than in most urban settings.

By the way, don't come here during the summer unless you have a good tent, bug spray, a hearty constitution, and a dash of craziness. The bugs here can be fierce. Winter is the best time. I've racked up at least 50 nights in this campground. My first trip took place during February, and I remember it like yesterday. I watched the sun sink over the palms and made a small fire. The hamburgers were delicious, and the stars overhead were a sight to behold. I bedded down early, then rose at first light, to see the land shrouded in fog.

Later, the day warmed, and I took an auto tour of the Big Cypress. Alligators and birds commanded the roadside canals. I bounced along the scenic Loop Road. Sunlight intermittently pierced the swamp, where the water was so clear it amazed me as much as the variety of bird life did. Anglers hung lazily on to cane poles wherever there was open water.

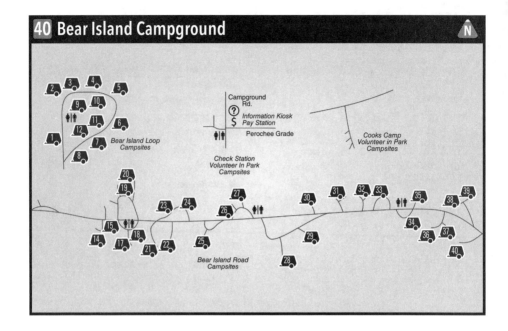

I walked a portion of the Florida National Scenic Trail. Here in the preserve, the Florida Trail starts its ultimate journey to northwest Florida. It begins right at the Big Cypress Visitor Center on US 41. Paddlers enjoy the Turner River, leaving from the ramp on US 41 near Everglades City, where outfitters are located.

Some people ride airboats in the preserve. Others drive big swamp buggies—you've got to see one to believe it. The Miccosukee Indians, who inhabit portions of the preserve, offer tourist rides for a fee in both of these vehicles. It is really a fun way to see a different part of this unique place.

Bear Island is your best bet for tent camping in the preserve. Make sure to bring all the water you will need. Big Cypress comprises the upper half of the Everglades ecosystem and is very different from most people's notions of what the Everglades look like. Camp at Bear Island and get to the bare essence of what tent camping is all about.

:: Getting There

From Everglades City, drive east on US 41 for 10 miles. Turn north on County Road 839 (Turner River Road) and follow it 19 miles, passing under I-75. Continue 1.3 miles beyond I-75 and turn right. Follow the gravel road 1.5 miles, passing the Wildlife Check-In Station on the way. The road will run into Bear Island Campground.

GPS COORDINATES   N26° 14′ 4.8″ W81° 16′ 59.0″

41

Caloosahatchee Regional Park Campground

The walk-in tent sites and recreation opportunities here should serve as a model for other tent-camping destinations.

This recreation area on the shores of the Caloosahatchee River is a favorite of mine. Not only does it have a great campground with excellent walk-in tent sites (and a few duds), but it also offers recreational opportunities that outdoor enthusiasts will enjoy. These include first-rate hiking trails directly adjacent to the campground, plus paddling opportunities not only in the Caloosahatchee River but also in nearby creeks that feed the river. Mountain bikers have an additional set of trails that they will find challenging. A manatee viewing area, known simply as Manatee Park, is on the way to the campground and is worth a stop.

Every site here is a walk-in tent site. Six of the 25 are for groups and are

:: Ratings

BEAUTY: ★ ★ ★ ★ ★
PRIVACY: ★ ★ ★ ★
SPACIOUSNESS: ★ ★ ★ ★ ★
QUIET: ★ ★ ★ ★
SECURITY: ★ ★ ★ ★ ★
CLEANLINESS: ★ ★ ★ ★ ★

intermingled with the rest of the campground. Follow the crushed shell path, which makes a loop through a gorgeous live oak hammock interspersed with open grassy areas. Don't worry about some of the sites being far—the park provides carts for toting gear from the parking area to the campsite. Massive live oaks topped with ferns, wild pineapple, and moss are the most notable trees in the campground. Palms and pines also grow tall overhead, while closer to the ground, clusters of palmetto and thick brush areas provide excellent privacy at most campsites. However, some of the campsites are situated in open grassy areas and are not desirable. Note the open outdoor showers spread throughout the campground. These are cold-water affairs, but hot showers are available at the bathhouse, where the restrooms are located.

Regulars will find their favorite sites and return to them year after year, as I do, while others will try to get sites closest to the parking lot. There are plenty of camps that offer the maximum in privacy and solitude. The campground fills on

:: Key Information

ADDRESS: 18500 North River Road Alva, FL 33920	**FACILITIES:** Hot and cold showers, flush toilets, water spigots
OPERATED BY: Lee County Parks and Recreation	**PARKING:** At designated parking area only
CONTACT: 239-693-2690; leegov.com/parks	**FEE:** $15/night
OPEN: Year-round	**ELEVATION:** 20′
SITES: 25	**RESTRICTIONS:**
EACH SITE: Picnic table, fire ring, upright grill	■ **Pets:** Prohibited
ASSIGNMENT: First come, first served; and by reservation	■ **Fires:** In fire grates only
	■ **Alcohol:** Prohibited
REGISTRATION: At ranger station	■ **Vehicles:** 2 vehicles/site
	■ **Other:** 2 tents/site

winter holiday weekends and occasionally on other nice-weather weekends when the air is cool and clear. Reservations are highly recommended during this time.

A set of nature trails, the Southside Trails, can be accessed from the campground. Follow a path to the day-use area, then pick up the 1.3-mile River Hammock Trail. It loops along the Caloosahatchee River after passing through the woods. The Palmetto Path travels 1.8 miles through the western part of the park. The Shoreline Trail travels along the river. The Overlook Trail leads 600 feet from the day-use area to a viewing area of the river and also to a fishing pier, which adds

to your recreational options. The North Side Trails can be accessed directly from the campground. Here you cross County Road 78 and get into some twisting and winding tracks that are multiple-use paths shared by equestrians and hikers but are primarily used by mountain bikers. The 10-plus miles will keep pedalers busy. Paddlers can rent kayaks from the park if they don't have their own. A kayak launch is located within walking distance of the campground. Boats can be rented by the hour or the day. You can paddle the Caloosahatchee River or explore Hickey Creek. Don't forget to view the manatees, at Manatee Park, located on FL 80.

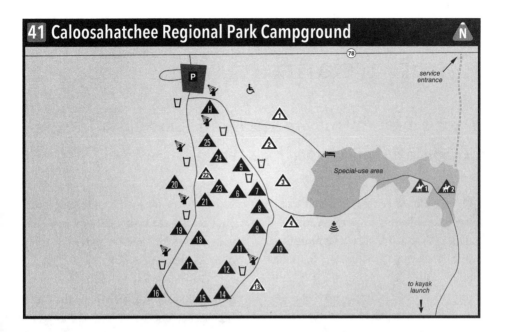

41 Caloosahatchee Regional Park Campground

:: Getting There

From Exit 141 on I-75 near Fort Myers, take FL 80 east 2.8 miles to FL 31. Turn left and take FL 31 north 2.7 miles to County Road 78, North River Road. You'll pass a left turn for CR 78 just after bridging the Caloosahatchee River. Ignore that left turn and keep forward on FL 31, passing the Lee County Civic Center; then turn right on CR 78 and follow it 7.8 miles to the campground entrance on your right. The first park entrance will be the North Side Trails parking area, on the left. Then you will pass the day-use area entrance on your right. The third entrance will be the campground entrance, on your right.

GPS COORDINATES   N26° 43' 24.5" W81° 38' 6.7"

42

Cayo Costa State Park Campground

*There is a sense of camaraderie here on Cayo Costa,
like you're all shipwrecked together.*

Cayo Costa is a barrier island that is accessible only by water. A trip here calls for a little planning, but it's more than worth it. If you like miles of unspoiled beaches, Gulf sunsets, and a tent-only campground, this is the place for you.

Your first step is to get a reservation on the ferry boat *Tropic Star*. Call 239-472-5100 to reserve your seat on the ferry. Then bring everything you will need for your camping trip. There is no store on the island and no convenient access to one once you are on it. Get to the ferry on time and enjoy the 90-minute ride from Pine Island to Cayo Costa.

Next, a park tram will take you from the bay side of the island to the Gulf side, where the campground is located. It's a

:: Ratings

BEAUTY: ★ ★ ★ ★ ★
PRIVACY: ★ ★ ★
SPACIOUSNESS: ★ ★ ★
QUIET: ★ ★ ★ ★ ★
SECURITY: ★ ★ ★ ★ ★
CLEANLINESS: ★ ★ ★ ★

little bothersome loading and unloading your gear on the boat and tram, but once you get set up, you'll wonder why you didn't get here sooner.

The tram drops you off at the campground. Resist the urge to run to the white beach and blue water; register for your campsite first. Follow the beachside sandy path running through a stand of Australian pines to a more open area of sea grape and other native plants. A hundred yards of sporadic sea oats divide you from the ocean. Campsites 1–3 are in the shade of the pines and look out on the Gulf.

The remaining 27 campsites are sunny overhead but are separated by rising thickets of sea grape. All of these sites feature an ocean view.

A spur path goes behind the small dune at campsite 5 to campsites 13–24. The sites are shielded from the wind, which makes them a little buggier but warm during infrequent cold spells. The beach vegetation, primarily sea grape and palm, provides adequate site privacy.

The other six campsites are on a path of their own amid some bigger thickets of

:: Key Information

ADDRESS: Cayo Costa State Park
P.O. Box 1150
Boca Grande, FL 33921

OPERATED BY: Florida State Parks

CONTACT: 941-964-0375, floridastate
parks.org; reservations 800-326-3521,
reserveamerica.com

OPEN: Year-round

SITES: 30 tent-only sites

EACH SITE: Picnic table, fire grate

ASSIGNMENT: Reservations required

REGISTRATION: By phone

FACILITIES: Showers, flush toilets,
piped water

PARKING: At marina; call ferry
service for schedule or visit
tropicstaradventures.com

FEE: $22/night

ELEVATION: Sea level

RESTRICTIONS:

■ **Pets:** Prohibited

■ **Fires:** In fire grates only

■ **Alcohol:** Prohibited

■ **Vehicles:** None allowed on island

■ **Other:** 14-day stay limit

sea grape. These sites are tucked away in the aforementioned thickets.

Three comfort stations serve the campground and 12 nearby cabins. Walk toward the cabins to the first comfort station. It has a shower, but it is in the open. This can be advantageous, when that afternoon sun warms you as the cold water runs down your back. The other comfort stations have enclosed showers for each sex on the outside of the building. All comfort stations have flush toilets and running sinks for each sex.

Winter is the time to come here. The sky is sunny, the breeze cool. The bugs are much less of a problem. It is not oppressively hot, as it can be in the summer. Bring bug repellent and a tent with fine mesh netting no matter what the season. Call ahead and ask about the insect conditions.

A sense of elation came over me as I got to the island. It was simply beautiful. Palm trees, live oaks, tall pines, and beach, beach, beach everywhere. I combed the beach first. Cayo Costa is known for its shelling. After storms, the beach is littered with all descriptions of shells. Next, I went for a swim. The Gulf waters here are clear and turquoise blue.

After my swim, I explored the five island trails on bicycle and foot. On these trails, you can see the old pioneer cemetery and the dense oak–palm hammocks in the center of the island. Next, I hiked to Quarantine Point and gazed out at the sailboats in the bay. An afternoon breeze kicked up as I walked the Gulf Trail, which runs for nearly 3 miles within sight of the beach. Sunbathers took in the rays. Some campers surf-fished for flounder, redfish, and snook. Others just strolled along the

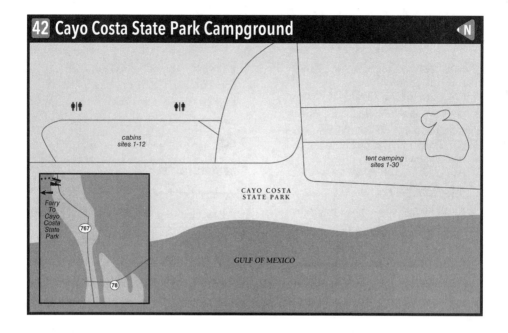

cabins
sites 1-12

tent camping
sites 1-30

CAYO COSTA
STATE PARK

Ferry
To
Cayo
Costa
State
Park

767

78

GULF OF MEXICO

beach, enjoying the ocean breeze. Later that evening, I ate supper with some new friends I had met on the ferry. Then we all took one last walk to watch the sunset. As if the day hadn't been magical enough, a full moon rose, illuminating the sea in brilliant points of light, as gentle waves lapped the shore.

Remember this: on the day of your return to the mainland, the ferry doesn't leave Cayo Costa until 1 p.m. Plan accordingly. I used my morning to walk the trails and to visit with my new friends. There is a sense of camaraderie here on Cayo Costa, like you're all shipwrecked together. I think everybody is extra friendly because they are so happy to be here. Come to Cayo Costa and you will have that feeling too.

:: Getting There

From North Fort Myers, take FL 78 for 16 miles to Pine Island. Turn right on String-fellow Road. After 6.2 miles, turn right on Barrancas Road, and then turn left onto Tortuga Street. The ferry to Cayo Costa departs from Jug Creek Marina, at 16498 Tortuga Street.

GPS COORDINATES   N26° 39' 47" W82° 14' 40"

43

DuPuis Campground

Camp in a tent-only venue and explore more than 20,000 acres of wildland in western Palm Beach County.

This is an underutilized South Florida inland resource. Leave the crowds on the beaches. The campground is situated in a pleasantly remote area. A raised crushed-shell road forms a loop around a shell–rock excavated pond. Overhead, a mix of palms and pines rises over grass. Some camps have but a single palm for shade, whereas others have multiple trees keeping the sun at bay. Palmetto islands divide many of the campsites. Of special note are campsites 13 and 14, which are situated on a little peninsula extending into the pond. Solar-powered vault toilets offer the latest in composting technology. Make sure to bring your own water. A bat house is located here to keep down the mosquitoes. A campground host, located at site 16, keeps things running smoothly. The

:: Ratings

BEAUTY: ★ ★ ★ ★
PRIVACY: ★ ★ ★
SPACIOUSNESS: ★ ★ ★ ★
QUIET: ★ ★ ★ ★ ★
SECURITY: ★ ★ ★
CLEANLINESS: ★ ★ ★

campground and trails are closed during managed hunts. Call ahead to make sure that the campground is open, especially during the winter. The management area visitor center is located a little west of the campground at Gate 5 on FL 76. The friendly folk will help you with any questions, either in person or on the phone.

Hiking is a huge draw here. A segment of the Ocean-to-Lake Trail, part of the Florida Trail system, travels through the management area. I enjoyed trekking this path, which winds through a mosaic of Florida ecosystems, from pine flatwoods to cypress domes. Gate 2 is a good starting area. Here you can take the trail leading south, which breaks up into three loops. The loop closest to Gate 1 is 4.3 miles long. A shorter loop hike starts at the Governor's House Picnic Area, just a little way beyond the campground on Jim Lake Grade. Here you can make a 2.8-mile loop. Pick up a trail map at the visitor center or check out the signboards at Gate 1. A blue-blazed trail leaves the campground next to a yellow-blazed equestrian trail and connects into the loop system. More than 40 miles of horseback paths traverse the

:: Key Information

ADDRESS: South Florida Water Management District, 3301 Gun Club Road, West Palm Beach, FL 33406	**REGISTRATION:** No registration
	FACILITIES: Vault toilet
	PARKING: At campsites only
OPERATED BY: South Florida Water Management District	**FEE:** None
	ELEVATION: 36'
CONTACT: 561-924-5310, sfwmd.gov	
OPEN: Year-round, closed during managed hunts	**RESTRICTIONS:**
	■ **Pets:** Prohibited
SITES: 16	■ **Fires:** In fire grates only
EACH SITE: Picnic table, fire ring	■ **Alcohol:** Prohibited
ASSIGNMENT: First come, first served; no reservations	■ **Vehicles:** None
	■ **Other:** Pack it in, pack it out

management area. Bicyclers like to pedal the old graded roads. Jim Lake Grade, the road that took you into the campground, is one. Another good pedal leads down DuPuis Grade to the fishing pier and picnic area in the southwest part of the management area. A partially covered fishing pier extends over a lake where you can angle for bass and bream, among other species. Whether you are pedaling or driving, the self-guided auto tour starts at Gate 1, which leads past the campground. Grab a brochure and enjoy the nine stops that also end at the fishing pier.

Stargazers from the Miami–Fort Lauderdale metroplex come out here, as it is far from city lights. And since no generators are allowed at the campground, it will be easy not only on the eyes but also on the ears. Campers have to create their own fun here, but the primitive remoteness of DuPuis is its biggest draw.

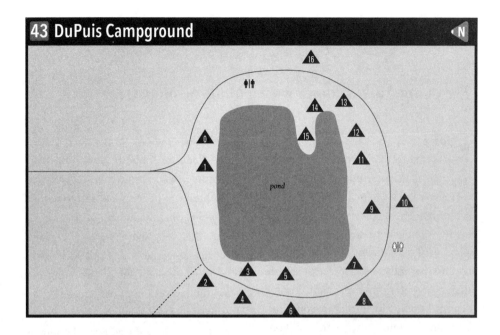

43 DuPuis Campground

:: Getting There

From Fort Lauderdale, take I-95 north to Exit 79, PGA Boulevard. Take PGA Boulevard west to FL 710. Take FL 710 north 12 miles to FL 76, Kanner Highway. Head west on FL 76 5.6 miles to Gate 1, the main entrance of DuPuis Wildlife Management Area. Turn left into Gate 1 and follow Jim Lake Grade 1 mile to the Family Campground, on your left. From Port Mayaca, on Lake Okeechobee, it is 6.3 miles on FL 76 to Gate 1.

GPS COORDINATES   N26° 59' 10.4" W80° 33' 5.4"

44

Elliott Key Campground

The campground comes with a million-dollar view.

Elliott Key is just one island of the many that make up Biscayne National Park, an exotic place of tropical forests and clear, rich waters. It seems somewhat out of place, being so close to the Miami metroplex. First declared a national monument in 1968, then a national park in 1980, this preserve is more than 95% water; however, there is some dry land upon which to pitch your tent. The campground comes with a million-dollar view. But the area came close to not having a campground at all. In the 1960s, a highway was slated to head down through this area. Conservationists banded together and stopped the highway from being built. However, before the land was turned over, developers cut a six-lane swath through the center of Elliott Key—a spiteful act of anger in not having the highway built. This swath

:: Ratings

BEAUTY: ★ ★ ★ ★
PRIVACY: ★ ★
SPACIOUSNESS: ★ ★ ★ ★
QUIET: ★ ★ ★ ★
SECURITY: ★ ★ ★ ★ ★
CLEANLINESS: ★ ★ ★ ★ ★

grew back, but park personnel have kept one "lane" of "Spite Highway" open for visitors to walk through a nicely recovering hardwood hammock, and to remind campers what might have been.

After your ferry ride to the island, set up camp and enjoy aquatic activities such as saltwater fishing, snorkeling, and swimming. The waters of Biscayne Bay are crystal clear and a sight to behold. Private boaters will have the additional option of diving and exploring many of the other Keys that make up the national park. However, on Elliott Key, there is Spite Highway to walk the tropical forest of the island's interior, where rare palms grow and rarer butterflies flutter in the springtime.

Elliott Key becomes visible as you chug over Biscayne Bay, the body of water that separates the Keys from the mainland. Land at Elliott Key dock, and the campground is visible off to your left. The sites are not numbered; camping is very casual here. A large grassy area lies between you and the dock. Most of the sites are shaded by tropical trees, such as gumbo-limbo, mahogany, and tamarind. The understory is mowed grass. The sites farthest from the ocean will have obscured views but more shade and privacy. The sites closest to the

:: Key Information

ADDRESS: Elliott Key Campground
9700 SW 328th St.
Homestead, FL 33033-5634

OPERATED BY: Biscayne National Park

CONTACT: 305-230-7275,
nps.gov/bisc

OPEN: Year-round

SITES: 15

EACH SITE: Picnic table, grill

ASSIGNMENT: First come, first served;
no reservations

REGISTRATION: Self-registration
on-site

FACILITIES: Showers, water spigots,
flush toilets

PARKING: At Convoy Point Visitor
Center

FEE: $25/night

ELEVATION: 2′

RESTRICTIONS:

■ **Pets:** On leash only

■ **Fires:** None

■ **Alcohol:** At campsites only

■ **Vehicles:** None allowed on island

■ **Other:** 14-day stay limit

ocean are more open and breezy, offering great views of Biscayne Bay. At those same sites, however, campers are visible to the day visitors who pull up to the dock. The sites closest to the water have easiest access to the nearby roped-off swim beach, which may be the finest natural pool you will ever enjoy.

Cold showers, water spigots, and flush toilets sit in a building on stilts near the camping area. Hurricanes pass this way in the fall, but that is no worry during the prime camping season here—winter. Winter is the best time to visit; otherwise, the mosquitoes will drive you crazy. Elliott Key fills up maybe one or two weekends per year. If you come during the week, you may have the campground all to yourself, like I did. The place is definitely underused.

Take a walk around Elliott Key. Start on the Elliott Key Trail, an interpretive walk that cuts through the heart of the narrow island from west to east. Along the way, you cross Spite Highway. If you take this trail north, you'll find good views of the Atlantic Ocean and the Gulf Stream in the distance. The Gulf Stream was a vital trade route in pre-engine days, and it comes perilously close to the Keys here. Many ships wrecked in the shallows off Elliott Key. This fact, combined with the clear waters and rich reefs, make diving out here popular. Landlubbers can choose to hike Spite Highway south to Petrel Point for ocean views and to see the remains of a residence that was part of a lime- and coconut-farming operation a century ago.

Boca Chita Key, just north of Elliott Key, has a short nature trail and

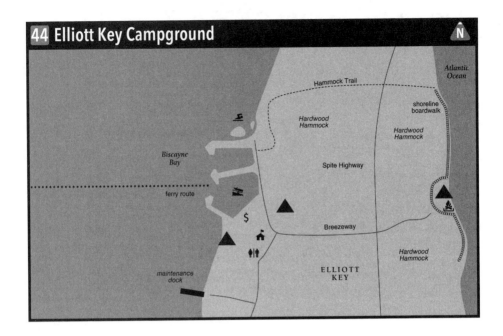

44 Elliott Key Campground

Atlantic Ocean

Hammock Trail

shoreline boardwalk

Hardwood Hammock

Hardwood Hammock

Biscayne Bay

Spite Highway

ferry route

Breezeway

$

Hardwood Hammock

ELLIOTT KEY

maintenance dock

a lighthouse that is open intermittently. The concessionaire boat lands here too. Adams Key is south of Elliott Key and has a short nature trail, but it's accessible only by private craft. The park has had troubles keeping concessionaires; call ahead for availability to see if a boat is running to Elliott Key. Or consider bringing your own boat. Kayakers regularly cross Biscayne Bay to overnight at Elliott Key. Do call and do come. This park won't disappoint.

:: Getting There

From Miami, head south on US 1 to Homestead and SW 328th Street. Turn left on SW 328th Street and follow the signs to Convoy Point Visitor Center.

GPS COORDINATES   N25° 26' 14" W80° 11' 52"

45

Flamingo Campground

Pitch your tent and go about the business of enjoying this unique ecosystem.

Flamingo was once a fishing village, cut off from the rest of Florida by the sea of saw grass known as the Everglades, accessible only by boat. Since that time, the park service has built a scenic road to Flamingo, which passes several Everglades attractions on the way to Florida Bay. Once here, you can pitch your tent and go about the business of enjoying this unique ecosystem.

Flamingo Campground is very large. There are more than 250 campsites in the entire campground. But the park service has kindly set aside a section for tent campers only. It has 40 campsites with an incredible ocean view. Being subdivided, Flamingo feels like three separate campgrounds rather than one huge one. Campers prefer to be in Flamingo

because it harbors the oceanic characteristics of the Everglades.

The main campground begins behind the registration booth. There are four loops. One loop is actually for trailers only; the other three are for RV and tent campers. Stay in the latter three loops if you must, but it is unlikely that the tent-only area will be full. The loop area has a smattering of palms and mahogany trees to break up the grassy understory.

Turn left beyond the registration booth to the walk-in tent area. Park your vehicle in the spaces provided for tent campers. The tenters' area lies between you and Florida Bay. The campsites are arranged by numbered sites in a somewhat hodgepodge fashion in a large grassy field, some 200 yards wide and 100 yards deep.

There is a complete lack of privacy between sites, except for the sheer distances of the campground. The campsites are placed well away from one another, with more room than you will need, especially since you carry your gear from car to campsite.

Fourteen campsites are directly on Florida Bay. A few trees lie on the oceanfront. These campsites overlook the small

:: Ratings

BEAUTY: ★ ★ ★ ★
PRIVACY: ★ ★ ★
SPACIOUSNESS: ★ ★ ★ ★ ★
QUIET: ★ ★
SECURITY: ★ ★ ★
CLEANLINESS: ★ ★ ★

:: Key Information

ADDRESS: Flamingo Campground 40001 FL 9336, Homestead, FL 33034

OPERATED BY: Everglades National Park

CONTACT: 305-242-7700, nps.gov /ever; reservations 877-444-6777, recreation.gov

OPEN: Year-round

SITES: 40 tent only; 270 total, including RV and group sites

EACH SITE: Tent area, stand-up fire grill, some RV sites have electricity

ASSIGNMENT: First come, first served; and by reservation

REGISTRATION: At registration booth

November–April; self-registration May–October

FACILITIES: Warm solar showers, flush toilet, water spigot

PARKING: At walk-in site parking lot

FEE: $20/night

ELEVATION: Sea level

RESTRICTIONS:
- **Pets:** On 6-foot leash maximum
- **Fires:** In grills only
- **Alcohol:** At campsites only
- **Vehicles:** None
- **Other:** 14 days total November–April; 30-day stay limit in calendar year

mangrove-covered keys dotting the bay. These small keys derive their name from the Spanish word cayo, meaning "island." The ocean views continually change with the time of day, but never, ever are they less than spectacular.

I was initially disappointed upon seeing the layout of this campground. But after getting acclimated to the openness of sky, field, and sea, I came to appreciate its unusual nature. The ocean breeze was welcome. Fellow tent campers I met shared stories of their experiences in the Everglades.

Comfort stations service this campground. Some provide warm water solar showers and flush toilets; the others have flush toilets only. The park service maintains a close eye for campers trying to sneak onto the field without paying, so be prepared to show your receipt.

Flamingo is best enjoyed during the winter season. Summer can be very rainy and very buggy. No matter when you come, bring a tent with adequate ventilation and netting. Bring long sleeves and long pants. Don't forget the bug dope!

Once settled in, walk to the Flamingo Visitor Center to get oriented. Here there are many ranger-led orientation programs. The ecosystem of the Everglades is an interesting story indeed. Sign up for a boat tour at the marina. Rent a motorboat and try your luck with rod and reel. Canoes and bicycles are available for rent there as well. Guided hikes and paddling trips are scheduled for the area. Check the local activity boards for your best bet.

If you like to discover the natural world on your own, there are ample opportunities. Hikers have eight excellent hikes from which to choose. Snake

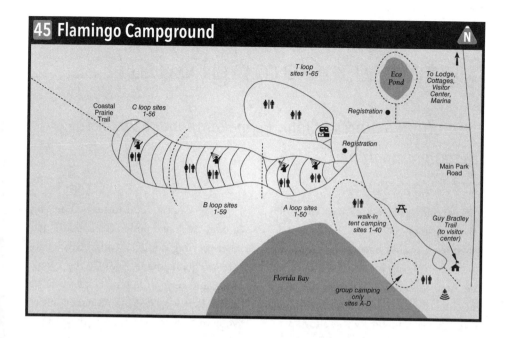

45 Flamingo Campground

T loop
sites 1-65

Eco
Pond

To Lodge,
Cottages,
Visitor
Center,
Marina

Coastal
Prairie
Trail

C loop sites
1-56

Registration

Registration

Main Park
Road

B loop sites
1-59

A loop sites
1-50

walk-in
tent camping
sites 1-40

Guy Bradley
Trail
(to visitor
center)

Florida Bay

group camping
only
sites A-D

Bight, Christian Point, and the Coastal Prairie trails are my favorites. Snake Bight exudes that tropical look and ends at a bird-watcher's boardwalk. Christian Point travels through multiple Everglades habitats. The Coastal Prairie Trail follows an old angler's path toward the unspoiled beaches of Cape Sable. Check at the visitor center for trailheads and directions.

Paddlers have seven water trails to explore in the immediate area. See alligators and crocodiles on the West Lake Trail. Paddle the narrow passageways of the Noble Hammock Trail. The Nine Mile Pond Trail makes a 5-mile loop through saw grass and mangroves. Canoes are sometimes available at the beginning of these trails, making rental easy. Again, inquire at the marina for information.

Flamingo can be anything you make it. Pick your campsite and jump into any of the activities that suit your fancy. Just make it back in time for sunset over Florida Bay.

:: Getting There

From US 1 in Florida City, follow the signs south to Everglades National Park. Flamingo Campground is 38 miles beyond the park entrance gate on the main park road.

GPS COORDINATES   N25° 8' 16.4" W80° 56' 23.3"

46

John Pennekamp Coral Reef State Park Campground

The natural features of John Pennekamp make up for the average campground.

This park protects part of the only living coral reef in the United States. The powers that be have made exploring this coral reef easy for everyone. Beware: the campground is nowhere near as enticing as the rest of the park, but you would never know it by the efforts you have to put forth to get a campsite here.

Just as the other state parks in the Keys, you are better off reserving a campsite up to 11 months in advance of your arrival. But once here, the campsite is yours for up to 14 days, as long as you renew it every day. You will still have to put up with some RVs. But because electricity is provided for each site, generator noise won't be a problem.

:: Ratings

BEAUTY: ★ ★ ★
PRIVACY: ★ ★
SPACIOUSNESS: ★ ★
QUIET: ★ ★
SECURITY: ★ ★ ★ ★
CLEANLINESS: ★ ★ ★

The campground forms a U around a tidal creek and pond. The sites are neither very big nor overly attractive. There are adequate shade trees at the campsites, and vegetation buffers between the sites are few. So don't jump naked out of your tent in the morning if this is your normal camping routine.

Campsites 1–22 abut the creek and pond. They generally have less vegetation than the sites on the other side of the campground. Campsites 23–40 run parallel to sites 1–22. They are backed against a thick stand of woods. Some of these have an adequate vegetation buffer offering a little more privacy. The final six sites follow the U back to the front of the campground.

Complete bathhouses are found at either end of the compact campground, affording easy access for all. This campground is not the greatest, but it will serve any tent camper who wants to check out what this state park has to offer.

Nearly 180 undersea nautical square miles are growing and waiting for you here under water. The clear, warm waters

:: Key Information

ADDRESS: John Pennekamp Coral Reef State Park Mile Marker 102.5, Overseas Highway Key Largo, FL 33037

OPERATED BY: Florida State Parks

CONTACT: 305-451-1202, floridastate parks.org; reservations 800-326-3521, reserveamerica.com

OPEN: Year-round

SITES: 46

EACH SITE: Picnic table, fire grill, water, electricity, sewer

ASSIGNMENT: First come, first served; assigned if reservations made

REGISTRATION: At entrance station

FACILITIES: Showers, flush toilets

PARKING: At campsites only

FEE: $36/night

ELEVATION: Sea level

RESTRICTIONS:

■ **Pets:** On leash only

■ **Fires:** In fire grates only

■ **Alcohol:** Prohibited

■ **Vehicles:** None

■ **Other:** 14-day stay limit

are alive with fish, turtles, lobsters, and plant life. Have you ever wanted to dive? There is an on-site dive shop that offers open-water certification for the novice, as well as advanced open-water certification for those who already know a thing or two about tanks and such. If that sounds like a little too much work, go snorkeling. It's easy with on-site equipment rental and guided tours of the reef. And if you would like to see the coral reef, but don't want to get wet, go on the glass-bottom boat tour.

Boat lovers can rent fishing boats, kayaks, canoes, paddleboards, and sailboats. All of these are ready to go at the marina in the center of the park. A 2.5-mile marked canoe trail winds through the park's mangrove wilderness. Maybe you want to see a fish at the end of your rod instead of on the coral reef. There are plenty here at John Pennekamp.

Sunbathers have two beaches to choose from. Far Beach is at the less-crowded, east end of the park. Cannon Beach is larger. It is by the main concession area. A roped-off swimming area makes it safer for families. A replica of an old Spanish galleon is located 130 feet off the shore of this beach, for divers to explore.

Landlubbers can check out the two nature trails. Step from the marina parking area onto the Wild Tamarind Trail and enter the forest that once covered much of the Keys. Visually, it's very stimulating; however, you can't escape the sounds of US 1. I enjoyed it nonetheless. Without this state park, even this small woodland would be a T-shirt shop.

Hike the Mangrove Trail. It is the only way you will ever get in the middle of a mangrove thicket without sinking up to your thighs in muck. That's because you

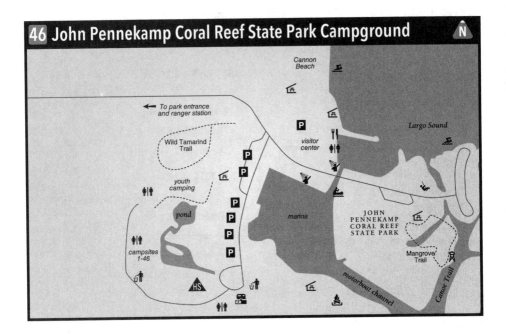

46 John Pennekamp Coral Reef State Park Campground

follow a boardwalk that has interpretive signs along the way to help you appreciate how a mangrove stand functions. I always enjoy these little trails. It helps me understand how every place is unique and is just one more strand in the intricate web of nature.

The natural features of John Pennekamp make up for the average campground. Don't pass this place by. And with all there is to do here, you will be too tired to care if it is not the world's finest place to set up a tent.

:: Getting There

To get there, look for John Pennekamp at mile marker 102.5 on US 1.

GPS COORDINATES   N25° 8′ 47″ W80° 23′ 12″

47

Jonathan Dickinson State Park Campground

The diversity of habitat and two campgrounds give you plenty of choices at Jonathan Dickinson State Park.

Jonathan **Dickinson** stumbled on this area when he was shipwrecked here in the late 1600s. You need only drive here to see what the southeast coast of Florida looked like before the massive development of today. There are two high-quality campgrounds from which to choose and a host of sights and activities to select from too.

The Pine Grove Camping Area stands near the park entrance. The Australian pines for which the camp is named are gone, courtesy of the hurricanes of the mid-2000s. But this is for the better, in my opinion, for the area has been replanted with native South Florida vegetation. However, the sites are much more open to the sun now, until the trees grow to full maturity. The camping area is laid out in a grid form, like city streets, beneath a dense canopy of nonnative Australian pines.

Two comfort stations are located here, one in the center of the camping grid and the other on the south end of the camping area. The sites on the outside of the grid are more open and sunny. Site spaciousness is not a problem anywhere.

The River Camping Area is near the remarkable Loxahatchee River, though no campsites are directly riverside. The River Camping Area houses more tent friendly campsites using the standard loop design, though most of the campsites are on the inside of the loop. Slash pines tower over the camping area. A heavy understory of palmetto divides the campsites, which are covered with well-maintained grass.

The buffers of palmetto provide maximum site privacy, but their overgrowth compromises site spaciousness in comparison with the Pine Grove Camping Area. A lone comfort station in the center of the loop serves the campground. This camping area is my favorite of the two. The flora is more developed, the campsite

:: Ratings

BEAUTY: ★ ★ ★
PRIVACY: ★ ★ ★
SPACIOUSNESS: ★ ★ ★
QUIET: ★ ★ ★
SECURITY: ★ ★ ★ ★
CLEANLINESS: ★ ★ ★

:: Key Information

ADDRESS: Jonathan Dickinson State Park, 16450 SE Federal Highway Hobe Sound, FL 33455	**FACILITIES:** Showers, flush toilets, soda machine
OPERATED BY: Florida State Parks	**PARKING:** At campsites and extra car parking area
CONTACT: 772-546-2771, floridastate parks.org; reservations 800-326-3521, reserveamerica.com	**FEE:** $26/night
OPEN: Year-round	**ELEVATION:** 20′
SITES: 135	**RESTRICTIONS:**
EACH SITE: Tent pad, picnic table, fire grill, water, electricity	■ **Pets:** On 6-foot leash only
ASSIGNMENT: Online or by ranger	■ **Fires:** In fire grates only
	■ **Alcohol:** Prohibited
REGISTRATION: By phone or at park entrance booth	■ **Vehicles:** None
	■ **Other:** 14-day stay limit

buffers are superior, and I like my sites a little more open.

After choosing your campground, what do you do? Start by learning more about the coastal sand pine scrub forest. It covers 20% of the park's 11,500 acres. This forest once covered much of the southeast coast of Florida. Now it is so rare that it is listed as a "globally imperiled" ecosystem.

Go directly to the Hobe Mountain observation tower. Mountains in Florida, you say? Here, the "mountains" are sandy hills that are cloaked in fast-disappearing pine scrub forest. It is a 5-minute walk up the boardwalk to the tower. Look over the Atlantic Ocean and the south of Florida. Natural views like this are unusual in the Sunshine State.

For a change of pace, check out the beautiful Loxahatchee River. There are two ways to do this. Self-motivators can rent a canoe and see for themselves the hardwood forest and cypress trees along the river. Keep your eyes peeled for alligators or a stray manatee. Or you can take the boat tour of the river aboard the *Loxahatchee Queen II*. It offers a 2-hour trip with an informative guide who will tell all the secrets of the river. It is hard to believe this park has two such different ecosystems so close together.

No matter how you get there, make sure to end up at Trapper Nelson's Place on the Loxahatchee River. It is only accessible by boat. Here you can learn about the man who came to this area to hunt and trap, earning the moniker "Wildman of the Loxahatchee." Explore his cabin and grounds, where he built his own wildlife zoo.

There are other things to do here as well. Bikers can pedal the park roads or enjoy their own special trail. Anglers can

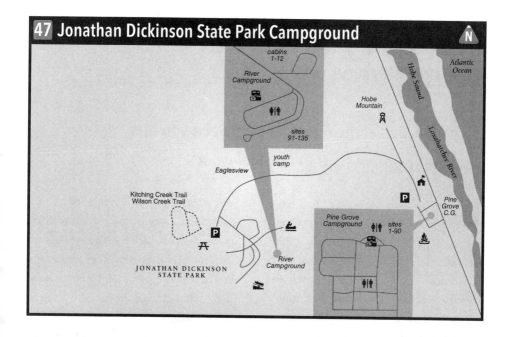

47 Jonathan Dickinson State Park Campground

cast a line for both saltwater and fresh-water species of fish. A section of the Ocean-to-Lake Trail winds through the coastal sand pine scrub forest. Use the East Loop Trail to bring you back to your starting point near the park entrance. The Kitching Creek Trail features a walk that explores yet more of this sizable state park.

The diversity of habitat and two campgrounds give you plenty of choices at Jonathan Dickinson State Park. First, make the choice to come here. But there is no need to wreck your ship to land in this piece of valuable Florida real estate.

:: Getting There

From Stuart, drive south on US 1 for 12 miles. Jonathan Dickinson State Park will be on your right.

GPS COORDINATES   N27° 1' 34.0" W80° 6' 36.1"

48

Long Key State Park Campground

A small beach is the only thing between you and your campsite, nestled in tropical woods.

Look out from your tent. Teal-blue waters extend as far as the eye can see. A small beach is the only thing between you and your campsite, nestled in tropical woods. The lovely waters of the Florida Keys are your playground here at Long Key State Park.

There is very little undeveloped land left in the Keys. Long Key State Recreation Area is just a sliver of the real Florida on a sliver of an island. But the 883 acres of "nonsubmergible" land packs a powerful punch. Of course, you'll want to explore the submergible land, enjoying the ocean above it.

Winter is Long Key's busy time. Make reservations if you know when you are coming. Do it up to 11 months before your planned arrival. Remember, you are guaranteed a campsite only for as many days as you have paid for. And, while we're discussing the downside, US 1 runs a little close to the campground. Unfortunately, in the land-starved Keys, everything is packed in tight.

Pass the entrance gate and turn right. The campground is to your left, between you and the Atlantic Ocean. All 60 sites run perpendicular to the ocean. Each campsite has its own oceanfront footage. Between each campsite is a vegetation buffer. And as the park's buffer restoration project continues, the buffers will become even thicker than they are today, which is adequately thick for site privacy.

Larger trees appear as the campsites run westerly. Sites 1–10 have shorter vegetation and are reserved for tent campers only. By the time you get to campsite 20, the tropical forest stands in full glory. Thankfully, the wooded buffer across from the campground shields some of the auto noise of US 1.

But don't let the traffic noise get to you; this campground is simply too scenic

:: Ratings

BEAUTY: ★ ★ ★ ★ ★
PRIVACY: ★ ★ ★
SPACIOUSNESS: ★ ★ ★
QUIET: ★ ★
SECURITY: ★ ★ ★
CLEANLINESS: ★ ★ ★|

:: Key Information

ADDRESS: Long Key State Park
67400 Overseas Highway
Long Key, FL 33001

OPERATED BY: Florida State Parks

CONTACT: 305-664-4815, floridastate
parks.org; reservations 800-326-3521,
reserveamerica.com

OPEN: Year-round

SITES: 60

EACH SITE: Tent pad, picnic table, fire
grill, electricity, ocean view

ASSIGNMENT: By reservation or
assigned by ranger

REGISTRATION: At entrance station

FACILITIES: Showers, flush toilets,
water spigots, electricity

PARKING: At campsites and
designated parking areas;
additional charge for extra cars

FEE: $36/night

ELEVATION: 7'

RESTRICTIONS:

- **Pets:** Prohibited
- **Fires:** In grills only
- **Alcohol:** Prohibited
- **Vehicles:** None
- **Other:** 14-day stay limit

to miss. And the ocean views—from your tent, from your picnic table, while you cook or read a magazine—they are what you imagine as you dream of warm, sunny days and breezy Keys nights. Just kick back and listen to the waves lap against the shoreline.

The three bathhouses are evenly spread throughout the campground. A single dump station with recycling bins serves all campers.

We arrived at Long Key on a rainy day. We set up a tarp and stir-fried shrimp obtained at a local fish market. The rain and the big meal lulled us into a nap. The rain had subsided when we awoke, so we decided to explore Long Key.

First, we hiked the hour-long Golden Orb Trail, which winds along the shoreline. From it, you can see the

Gulf Stream flowing 4 miles out at sea. Close views include mangrove thickets and salt-intolerant hardwood hammocks that grow only at the highest points in the Keys. Steam rose from the sand in the open woods away from the beach.

Next, we grabbed the canoe and paddled the Long Key Lakes Canoe Trail. It starts near the park entrance. We followed the numbered posts, learning more about tidal lagoons, the "nurseries of the sea." These tidal lagoons are the beginning of the ocean food chain for creatures of the sea and for birds. The clouds broke and a rainbow appeared—a sign of good luck.

Another hiking trail at Long Key is the quarter-mile Layton Trail. It starts across US 1 and explores the tropical forest and shoreline of the Gulf side of Long

48 Long Key State Park Campground

Key. There is a fine swimming beach next to the picnic area.

Other activities center on the beautiful Atlantic waters. Flats fishing or deep-water fishing, snorkeling, and shelling keep campers busy. We watched a fantastic Keys sunset and kicked back at our campsite, just taking in the breeze. After you get your campsite, you have nothing left to worry about in this laid-back campground.

:: Getting There

To get there, look for Long Key State Recreation Area at mile marker 67.5 on US 1.

GPS COORDINATES   N24° 49' 0.5" W80° 49' 12.2"

49

Long Pine Key Campground

Long Pine Key Campground has a pace as slow as the waters that flow through the river of saw grass that is the Everglades.

Set in a forest of fragrant southern slash pine, Long Pine Key Campground has a pace as slow as the waters that flow through the river of saw grass that is the Everglades. But another important plant community thrives here: pine flatwoods. These pines grow on limestone that was once an ancient coral reef.

This campground is part of an area known as the Pinelands. The 108 campsites stretch around one side of a quiet lake. A picnic area lies on the other side. The campsites, 11 in all, are situated on an elongated loop with crossroads that connect one side of the loop to the other.

Most of the campsites are located along these 11 crossroads. The spacious sites are divided by the understory of the pine flatwoods—primarily saw palmetto

and hardwood seedlings. These hardwood seedlings would grow and alter the forest from pine to hardwood, but lightning-caused fires destroy the undergrowth, and the mature pines' tough bark is able to withstand the periodic fires.

The lakeview campsites are the most desirable. By the way, swimming is not allowed in the lake—I assume it is because of alligators. The campground is rarely full, save for the winter holidays. Winter is the busiest, most pleasant time to be here. It is the dry season in the Everglades, and the bug population is minimal. But there will be others at Long Pine Key in their RVs, escaping the chill of the North.

I stayed at one of the sites on the outside of the loop, facing the piney woods. Like the other sites here, mine offered a grassy, mowed lawn, with the maximum in spaciousness and an acceptable amount of privacy. I enjoyed looking over the tall pines and smelling their distinct odor while gathering firewood.

Three clean comfort stations, with water spigots outside each one, serve the well-kept campground. There is also a

:: Ratings

BEAUTY: ★ ★ ★ ★
PRIVACY: ★ ★ ★
SPACIOUSNESS: ★ ★ ★ ★ ★
QUIET: ★ ★
SECURITY: ★ ★ ★
CLEANLINESS: ★ ★ ★ ★

:: Key Information

ADDRESS: Long Pine Key
40001 FL 9336
Homestead, FL 33034

OPERATED BY: Everglades
National Park

CONTACT: 305-242-7700,
nps.gov/ever

OPEN: Year-round

SITES: 108

EACH SITE: Picnic table, fire pit

ASSIGNMENT: First come, first served;
no reservations

REGISTRATION: At campground
registration booth November–April;
self-registration May–October

FACILITIES: Flush toilets, water spigots

PARKING: At campsites only

FEE: $20/night

ELEVATION: 4'

RESTRICTIONS:

- Pets: On 6-foot leash maximum
- Fires: In fire pits only
- Alcohol: At campsites only
- Vehicles: None
- Other: 14 days total November–
April; 30-day stay limit in calendar
year

large washbasin at each comfort station. A campground host mans the entrance for your safety. The only things you should be wary of are the raccoons. Store your food properly or these critters will get your groceries when you leave. And leave you must, to explore the unique Everglades.

Road-weary campers need only step away from the campground to see the Pinelands. A set of interconnecting trails open to hikers and bicyclers emanates from Long Pine Key. The backbone of the trail system is the 6.7-mile Long Pine Key Nature Trail. It winds through the pine flatwoods, saw grass prairie, and hardwood hammocks, ending near Pine Glades Lake.

These hardwood hammocks are islands of tropical plant life, with wild palms, mahogany trees, and live oaks. There are nearly 20 miles of trails to tramp in the immediate area of the campground. Get a trail map at the registration booth and make your own loop.

Two of the park's premier interpretive footpaths, Gumbo Limbo and Anhinga trails, are just a short drive away at the Royal Palm Visitor Center. The Gumbo Limbo Trail leads through a hardwood hammock that features flora of the West Indies, such as gumbo-limbo, royal palm, ferns, and vines, which all lend to a junglelike atmosphere. The Anhinga Trail is a scenic boardwalk on the sea of saw grass leading to Taylor Slough, a wildlife photographer's paradise. A plethora of birds, alligators, and other creatures dwells in this portion of the Everglades.

Auto tourists can drive to the Pa-hay-okee Overlook, west of Long Pine Key. Climb the observation tower and look around. The sky, the saw grass, and the hardwood hammocks extend to the

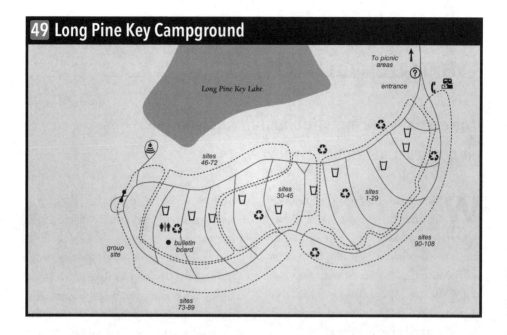

49 Long Pine Key Campground

horizon. We drove here for a dramatic sunrise. A few miles west on the main road is Mahogany Hammock. It contains the largest mahogany tree in America, as well as a menagerie of unusual flora and fauna.

No matter where you go in the Everglades, don't rush. Stop, look, listen. This is a unique ecosystem, unlike any other on our planet. Its beauty is expansive and subtle, intricate and fragile. Here, life proceeds at its own pace. Leave the hurried world behind, make Long Pine Key your base camp, and get on Everglades time.

:: Getting There

From US 1 in Homestead, follow the signs south along FL 9336 to Everglades National Park. Stay on the main park road. The signed turn to Long Pine Key is 6 miles beyond the park visitor center. Turn left and drive 0.5 mile to the campground.

GPS COORDINATES   N25° 24' 5.2" W80° 39' 19.8"

50

Oscar Scherer State Park Campground

The area's best campground, offering creekside campsites and ample privacy

When you combine the outdoor features of Myakka River, Oscar Scherer, and Casey Key, you get a full plate of southwest Florida landscape with enough activities to wear you out daily. The campground at Oscar Scherer is the area's best, offering creekside campsites and ample privacy.

South Creek flows lazily through Oscar Scherer's 1,384 acres. You cross the creek on a small bridge to access the campground, which stretches along the shaded creek bank, forming a narrow loop divided by four access roads.

Turn left after crossing the bridge. Sixteen creekside sites are on your left. Dense undergrowth keeps each site private. Tenters will favor these shaded sites.

:: Ratings

> BEAUTY: ★ ★ ★
> PRIVACY: ★ ★ ★
> SPACIOUSNESS: ★ ★ ★
> QUIET: ★ ★
> SECURITY: ★ ★ ★ ★
> CLEANLINESS: ★ ★ ★ ★

After you pass a footbridge, there is a spur road with four secluded creekside campsites.

Fourteen campsites lie away from the creek as the loop doubles back. These sites have privacy-yielding undergrowth, though shade trees are fewer than the creekside sites. Past the campfire circle are 26 more sites having the same buffer vegetation of the scrubby flatwoods.

Six drive-through sites are for RVs only as the loop doubles back again to border South Creek. Again, overhead shade becomes abundant. The final 31 creekside sites are among the first to go when this campground fills. Little footpaths course throughout the woods to five bathhouses conveniently dispersed in the narrow loop's center. Each bathhouse has a hot shower for each sex.

This campground may sound large, but so much vegetation has been left intact. Campers can see only a few sites other than their own, making it seem more intimate. Expect a few RVs, but electrical hookups at each site mean no generators to keep you awake. The busy

:: Key Information

ADDRESS: Oscar Scherer State Park
1843 South Tamiami Trail
Osprey, FL 34229

OPERATED BY: Florida State Parks

CONTACT: 941-483-5956, floridastate
parks.org; reservations 800-326-3521,
reserveamerica.com

OPEN: Year-round

SITES: 104

EACH SITE: Tent pad, picnic table, fire
ring, water, electricity

ASSIGNMENT: Online, by phone, or
first come, first served

REGISTRATION: Ranger registration
on site

FACILITIES: Showers, flush toilets

PARKING: At campsites and in extra
car parking areas

FEE: $26/night

ELEVATION: 5'

RESTRICTIONS:
- **Pets:** On 6-foot leash maximum
- **Fires:** In fire rings only
- **Alcohol:** Prohibited
- **Vehicles:** Limit 2 vehicles/site
- **Other:** 14-day stay limit

season is from November through May. Reservations are suggested for that time.

Once you get a site, you probably won't be there much. South Creek has both paddling and saltwater-fishing opportunities. Canoes, single kayaks, and double kayaks can be rented at the ranger station. Two short nature trails, the Lester Finley Barrier Free Trail and South Creek Trail, run along the creek across from the campground. Lake Osprey, a freshwater lake, is a great place for swimming.

Oscar Scherer is home to two threatened plant communities, pine flatwoods and scrubby flatwoods. This high, dry, easily developed land is being cut down all over the state. But this protected tract has more than 15 miles of interconnected trails for you to hike. The trails are generally easy and level. The White Trail is of particular note, circling South Creek

as it flows out of the north. We are lucky Oscar Scherer's daughter, Elsa Scherer Burrows, donated this diminishing landscape for us to enjoy.

Nearby Myakka River State Park contains more than 28,000 acres of the real Florida landscapes. It has unique plant and animal communities too. By the way—the campground at Myakka River is cramped, open, and has too many RVs for me. But a trip here is worth the half-hour drive from Oscar Scherer. Why? Prairies, rivers, lakes, trails, and wildlife.

The Myakka River is the park's centerpiece. The river flows through the park and widens to become Upper Myakka Lake. Both bodies of water are suitable for canoeing and fishing. If you like tours, there is an airboat tour of the lake and a tram tour covering part of the park's 45 square miles.

50 Oscar Scherer State Park Campground

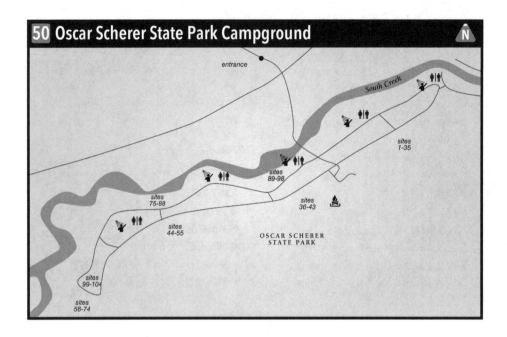

The adventurous may want to explore the backcountry here. Foot trails lace the park, passing oak hammocks, numerous ponds, and Florida's prairie lands. These prairies are remnants of 300,000 acres of prairie land that once covered the state's interior. Grasses, wildflowers, and palmetto cover this unique ecosystem that was kept clear by lightning-induced fires.

Alligators are plentiful in this park and can be viewed during winter months. Deer, bobcats, and other wildlife also live here in abundance. Myakka River hosts a large population of birds, and the lakeside boardwalk is a great start for birders.

After you have exhausted yourself, hit the beach. It is a short drive down US 41 to the public beach on Casey Key. Here, you can relax by the beautiful Gulf waters and white sands. Then you will have enjoyed a full taste of Florida's southwest, with Oscar Scherer as your headquarters.

:: Getting There

Oscar Scherer State Park is just south of Osprey on US 41.

GPS COORDINATES   N27° 10′ 25.9″ W82° 28′ 14.2″

APPENDIX A

● ●

Camping-Equipment Checklist

Except for the large and bulky items on this list, I keep a plastic storage container full of the essentials of car camping so that they're ready to go when I am. I make a last-minute check of the inventory, resupply anything that's low or missing, and away I go!

COOKING UTENSILS

Bottle opener
Bottles of salt, pepper, spices, sugar, cooking oil, and maple syrup in water-proof, spill-proof containers
Can opener
Cups, plastic or tin
Dish soap (biodegradable), sponge, towel
Flatware
Food of your choice
Frying pan
Fuel for stove
Matches in waterproof container
Plates
Pocketknife
Pot with lid
Spatula
Stove
Tin foil
Wooden spoon

FIRST-AID KIT

Adhesive bandages
Aspirin or ibuprofen
First-aid cream
Gauze pads
Insect repellent
Moleskin
Snakebite kit
Sunscreen and lip balm
Tape, waterproof adhesive

SLEEPING GEAR

Pillow
Sleeping bag
Sleeping pad, inflatable or insulated
Tent with ground tarp and rainfly

MISCELLANEOUS

Bath soap (biodegradable), washcloth, and towel
Camp chair
Candles
Cooler
Deck of cards
Fire starter
Flashlight with fresh batteries
Foul-weather clothing
GPS
Lantern
Maps (road, topographic, trails, and so on)
Paper towels
Plastic zip-top bags
Sunglasses
Toilet paper
Water bottle
Wool blanket

OPTIONAL

Barbecue grill
Binoculars
Field guides on bird, plant, and wildlife identification
Fishing rod and tackle
Hatchet

APPENDIX B

● ●

Sources of Information

The following is a partial list of agencies, associations, and organizations to write or call for information on outdoor recreation opportunities in Florida.

APALACHICOLA NATIONAL FOREST
www.fs.usda.gov/apalachicola

APALACHICOLA RANGER DISTRICT
11152 NW FL 20
Bristol, FL 32321
850-643-2282

BIG CYPRESS NATIONAL PRESERVE
33100 Tamiami Trail E
Ochopee, FL 34141
239-695-2000
nps.gov/bicy

BISCAYNE NATIONAL PARK
9700 SW 328th St.
Homestead, FL 33033-5634
305-230-1144
nps.gov/bisc

**DEPARTMENT OF
ENVIRONMENTAL PROTECTION**
Division of Recreation and Parks
Mail Station #535
3900 Commonwealth Blvd.
Tallahassee, FL 32399-3000
850-245-2118

EVERGLADES NATIONAL PARK
40001 FL 9339
Homestead, FL 33034-6733
305-242-7700
nps.gov/ever

FLORIDA DIVISION OF FORESTRY
3125 Conner Blvd.
Tallahassee, FL 32399-1650
850-488-4274

FLORIDA DIVISION OF TOURISM
Collins Building
107 W Gaines St.
Tallahassee, FL 32301
888-735-2872
visitflorida.com/en-us.html

LAKE GEORGE RANGER DISTRICT
17147 E FL 40
Silver Springs, FL 34488
352-625-2520

OCALA NATIONAL FOREST
www.fs.usda.gov/ocala

OSCEOLA NATIONAL FOREST
P.O. Box 70
Olustee, FL 32072
386-752-2577
www.fs.usda.gov/osceola

SEMINOLE RANGER DISTRICT
40929 FL 19
Umatilla, FL 32784
352-669-3153

WAKULLA RANGER DISTRICT
1773 Crawfordville Highway
Crawfordville, FL 32327
850-926-3561

INDEX

● ●

A

Adams Key, 144
Alafia River, 117, 118-119
Alexander Springs Creek canoe run, 91
Alexander Springs Recreation Area
  Campground, 90-92
Alexander Springs Wilderness, 91
Amelia Island, 72
Amelia Island State Park, 70
Amelia River, 61-62
Anastasia State Park Campground, 58-60
Anclote River, 123
Apalachee Savannahs Scenic Byway, 55
Apalachicola, 45-46
Apalachicola National Forest, 164
Apalachicola River, 18, 50, 52, 54-55
Apalachicola River Bluffs Trail, 51

B

Bahia Honda State Park Campground,
  127-129
Bartram, William, 75
bathrooms, 6
beach campgrounds, best, xii
Bear Island Campground, 130-132
beauty, rating system, 1
best campgrounds, xi-xii
bicyclers, best campgrounds for, xi
Big Cypress National Preserve, 130, 164
Big Gum Swamp Wilderness, 81
Big Lagoon State Park Campground, 8-10
Big Lake Johnson, 66
Big Talbot Island State Park Campground, 70
Biscayne Bay, 142, 143, 144
Biscayne National Park, 142, 164
Blackwater River State Park Campground,
  11-13
Blue Hole Camping Area, Florida Caverns
  State Park, 23, 25

Blue Spring State Park Campground, 93-95
Boca Chita Key, 143-144
book, about this, 3-6
Burrows, Elsa Scherer, 161

C

Caloosahatchee Regional Park
  Campground, 133-135
Caloosahatchee River, 133, 134
Calusa Beach, Bahia Honda, 128
Camel Lake Campground, 14-16
campground profiles, 2
campgrounds. See also specific campground
  best, i-xii
  in Central Florida, 89-125
  in Florida's Panhandle, 7-55
  GPS entrance coordinates, 3
  maps, 2
  in Northern Florida, 57-88
  in South Florida, 126-162
camping
  equipment checklist, 163
  etiquette, 4-5
  sources of information, 164
  tips for happy trips, 5-6
Casey Key, 160, 162
Cayo Costa State Park Campground,
  136-138
Central Florida campgrounds, 89-125
Chain of Lakes Trail, Blackwater River State
  Park, 12
Chassahowitzka River, 96, 97
Chassahowitzka River Campground,
  Indian Ridge Loop, 96-98
Chassahowitzka River National Wildlife
  Refuge, 96, 97
Chipola River, 18, 23

C (Continued)

Civil War sites, 62–63, 80, 85, 87
cleanliness, rating system, 2
Clearwater Lake Campground, 99–101
Coldwater Creek, Blackwater River State
 Park, 12, 13
Cone's Dike, 83
Crooked Creek Trail, 36–37

D

Dead Lakes Park Campground, 17–19
Dead River, 33
Deer Lake, 66
Dickinson, Jonathan, 151
DuPuis Campground, 139–141
Duval Street, Key West, 128

E

East Lake, 35
Edgar "Dutch" Tiemann Nature Trail, 36–37
Elliott Key Campground, 142–144
equipment checklist, camping, 163
Everglades ecosystem, 132, 146–147, 157
Everglades National Park, 164

F

Falling Water Sink, 21
Falling Waters State Park Campground,
 20–22
ferry boat *Tropic Star*, 136
first-aid kits, 4, 163
fishing, best campgrounds for, xi
Flamingo Campground, 145–147
Floodplain Trail, Florida Caverns
 State Park, 24
Florida
 campgrounds in Central, 89–125
 campgrounds in Northern, 57–88
 campgrounds in Panhandle, 7–55
 campgrounds in South, 126–162
Florida Caverns State Park Campground,
 23–25
Florida National Scenic Trail, 14–15, 37, 65,
 80, 92, 100, 108, 113, 131–132

Florida's Panhandle campgrounds, 7–55
For George Island State Park, 70
Fore Lake, 115
Fort Braden, Western Lake, 30
Fort Clinch, 62–63
Fort Clinch State Park Campground, 61–63
Fort Gadsden Historic Site, 55
Fort Matanzas National Monument, 60

G

Gaines-Hawthorne Trail, 84
Gold Head Branch State Park Campground,
 64–66
GPS campground-entrance coordinates, 3
Grayton Beach State Park Campground, 26–28
Gregory House, 50, 51
guidebook, how to use this, 1–3
Gulf Stream, 143

H

Hammock Campground at Jennings State
 Forest, 67–69
Hemingway, Ernest, 128
Henderson Beach State Recreation Area,
 39–40
Hickey Creek, 134
High Bluff Campground, 29–31
hiking, best campgrounds for, xi
Hillsborough River Hiking Trail, 103
Hillsborough River State Park Campground,
 102–104
Hobe Mountain observation tower, 152
Hog Island Recreation Area Campground,
 105–107
Homosassa Springs State Wildlife Park,
 118, 122
Hopkins Prairie Campground, 108–110

I

Ichetucknee Springs State Park, 78
Indian Ridge Loop, Chassahowitzka River
 Campground, 96–98
information, sources of, 164
island campgrounds, best, xii

J

Jennings State Forest, 67–69
John Gorrie Museum, Apalachicola, 46
John Pennekamp Coral Reef State Park
    Campground, 148–150
Jonathan Dickinson State Park
    Campground, 151–153
Juniper Creek, Blackwater River State Park,
    12, 13
Juniper Prairie Wilderness, 113
Juniper Springs Recreation Area
    Campground, 111–113
Juniper Wayside Park, 112

K

kayak rentals, 12
Keno, 76
Key West, 128

L

lake campgrounds, best, xi
Lake Eaton Campground, 114–116
Lake George, 112–113
Lake Lou, 115
Lake Talquin, 29
Lake Wauberg, 82
layout maps, 2
legend, map, 2
Leon, Ponce de, xiv
Lines Tract trails, 30
Lithia Springs Park Campground, 117–119
Little Lake Johnson, 65, 66
Little Talbot Island State Park Campground,
    70–72
Little Withlacoochee River, 106
Logger Head Beach, Bahia Honda, 128
Long Island State Park, 70
Long Key State Park Campground, 154–156
Long Key State Recreation Area, 154
Long Pine Key Campground, 157–159
Loxahatchee Queen II riverboat, 152

M

Mahogany Hammock, 159

Mallory Square, Key West, 128
Manatee Park, 133, 134
Manatee Springs State Park Campground,
    73–75
maps. See also specific campground
    campground, layout, 2
    overview, key, legend, 2
Memery Island, 15
Miccosukee Indians, 132
Miss Maggie's campground, 96
Molloy, Johnny, xiv, 169
Mount Cornelia, 71
Mutual Mine Recreation Area Campground,
    120–122
Myakka River, 160, 162
Myakka River State Park, 161

N

Nine Mile Creek, 92
North Fork Black Creek, 67–68
Northern Florida campgrounds, 57–88

O

Ocala National Forest, 92, 99, 108, 111,
    113, 115
Ocean Pond Campground, 79–81
Ocean-to-Lake Trail, Palm Beach County, 139
Ochlockonee River, 32–33
Ochlockonee River State Park Campground,
    32–34
Ocklawaha River, 115
O'Leno State Park Campground, 76–78
Olustee Battlefield, 80
Oscar Scherer State Park Campground,
    160–162
Osceola National Forest, 79, 80, 81, 100, 164

P

paddling, best campgrounds for, xi
Paisley Woods Bicycle Trail, 100
Palmetto islands, 123, 139
Panama City Beach, 35
Paynes Prairie Preserve State Park
    Campground, 82–84
Pebble Lake, 66

P *(Continued)*

Peck, Gregory, 109
Perdido Key Recreation Area, 8, 9–10
Petrel Point, Elliott Key, 143
Pine Glades Lake, 158
Pine Log Creek, 35, 36
Pine Log State Forest Campground, 35–37
Pinelands, 157–158
Pithlachasotee River, 123, 124
Ponce de Leon, xiv
privacy, rating system, 1
Puddin' Head Lake, 38

Q

Quarantine Point, Cayo Costa, 137
quiet, rating system, 2

R

rating system, 1–2
Rawlings, Marjorie Kinnan, 109
river campgrounds, best, xi–xii
Rocky Bayou Aquatic Preserve, 39
Rocky Bayou State Park Campground, 38–40
Royal Palm Visitor Center, 158

S

Sandspur Beach, Hahai Honda, 128
Santa Fe River, 76, 77–78
Second Seminole War, 104
security, rating system, 2
Seminole Indian Wars, 102, 104
Shady Pines Camp, St. Joseph Peninsula
   State Park Campground, 47–48
Sheeler Lake, 66
Shell Island, 42–43
Silver Glen Springs, 109
Silver Lake, 106
Sinkhole Trail, Falling Waters State Park, 21
solitude, best campgrounds for, xi
South Florida campgrounds, 126–162
spaciousness, rating system, 1
Spite Highway, 142, 143
St. Andrews State Park Campground, 41–43
St. Augustine, 60
St. George Island, 44
St. George Island State Park Campground,
   44–46

St. Johns River, 71, 91, 93, 94, 95
St. Joseph Peninsula State Park
   Campground, 47–49
St. Marks National Wildlife Refuge, 32,
   33–34
star rating system, 1–2
Starkey, Jay B., 123
Starkey Wilderness Park Campground,
   123–125
Sumatra, 55
Suwannacoochee Camp Area, 85
Suwannee River, 73, 74, 85, 86
Suwannee River State Park Campground,
   85–88
Sweetwater Creek, Blackwater River State
   Park, 12, 13

T

Taylor Slough, Long Pine Key, 158
tent-camping in Florida, 3
tents, pitching, 6
Terrace Trail, Falling Waters State Park,
   21
Thursby House, 94
Timucuan Indians, 90, 92
toilets, 6
Torreya State Park Campground,
   50–52
Tropic Star ferry boat, 136
Turner River, 132

U

Upper Myakka Lake, 161

W

Wakulla Springs, 33–34
Weeping Ridge Camping Area, 50
Western Lake, 26, 27
wildlife watching, best campgrounds for, xi
Withlacoochee River, 85, 87, 106
Withlacoochee State Forest, 105, 121
Wright Lake, 53, 54
Wright Lake Recreation Area Campground,
   53–55

Y

Yearling, The (Rawlings), 108

ABOUT THE AUTHOR

Johnny Molloy is an outdoor writer based in Johnson City, Tennessee. Born in Memphis, he moved to Knoxville in 1980 to attend the University of Tennessee (UT). During his college years, he developed a love of the natural world that has since become the primary focus of his life.

It all started on a backpacking foray into the Great Smoky Mountains National Park. That first trip was a disaster; still, Johnny discovered an affinity for the outdoors that would lead him to backpack and canoe-camp throughout the United States over the next 25 years. Today, he averages 150 nights out per year.

After graduating from UT with a degree in economics, Johnny spent an ever-increasing amount of time in the wild, becoming more skilled in a variety of environments. Friends enjoyed his adventure stories; one even suggested that he write a book. He pursued that idea and soon parlayed his love of the outdoors into an occupation.

The results of his efforts are more than 30 books. These include hiking, camping, paddling, and other comprehensive guidebooks, as well as books on true outdoor adventures. Johnny has also written for numerous publications and websites. He continues to write and travel extensively to all four corners of the United States, exploring a variety of outdoor activities. For the latest on Johnny, please visit johnnymolloy.com.

DEAR CUSTOMERS AND FRIENDS,

SUPPORTING YOUR INTEREST IN OUTDOOR ADVENTURE, travel, and an active lifestyle is central to our operations, from the authors we choose to the locations we detail to the way we design our books. Menasha Ridge Press was incorporated in 1982 by a group of veteran outdoorsmen and professional outfitters. For many years now, we've specialized in creating books that benefit the outdoors enthusiast.

Almost immediately, Menasha Ridge Press earned a reputation for revolutionizing outdoors- and travel-guidebook publishing. For such activities as canoeing, kayaking, hiking, backpacking, and mountain biking, we established new standards of quality that transformed the whole genre, resulting in outdoor-recreation guides of great sophistication and solid content. Menasha Ridge Press continues to be outdoor publishing's greatest innovator.

The folks at Menasha Ridge Press are as at home on a whitewater river or mountain trail as they are editing a manuscript. The books we build for you are the best they can be, because we're responding to your needs. Plus, we use and depend on them ourselves.

We look forward to seeing you on the river or the trail. If you'd like to contact us directly, visit us at menasharidge.com. We thank you for your interest in our books and the natural world around us all.

SAFE TRAVELS,

Bob Sehlinger

BOB SEHLINGER
PUBLISHER